The Indians of Yellowstone Park

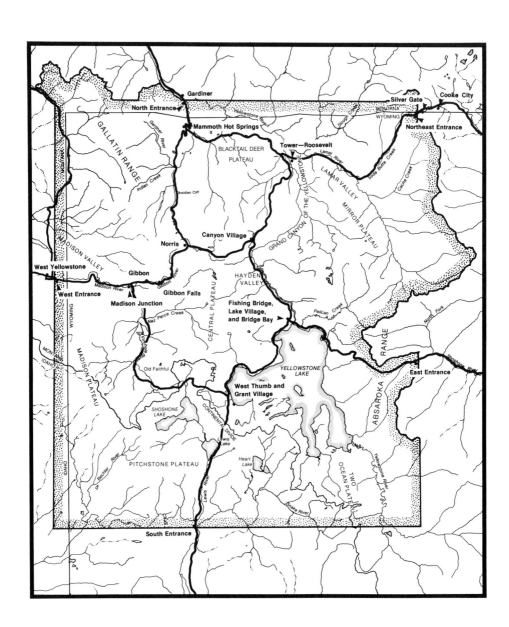

The Indians *of* Yellowstone Park

JOEL C. JANETSKI

Bonneville Books
University of Utah Press
Salt Lake City
1987

Library of Congress Cataloging-in-Publication Data

Janetski, Joel C.
The Indians of Yellowstone Park.

(Bonneville books)
Bibliography: p.
Includes index.
1. Indians of North America—Wyoming.
2. Indians of North America—Yellowstone National Park.
3. Yellowstone National Park.   I. Title.
E78.W95J36   1987   978.7'5200497   86–28295
ISBN 0–87480–272–5

Cover illustration by Charles M. Bell,
Bureau of American Ethnology, Smithsonian Institution

8-27-87

Contents

Maps

Chart

Illustrations

The Indians of Yellowstone Park

1

The Land

For thousands of years man has lived in, traveled through, and exploited the vast pine-covered plateau now known as Yellowstone Park. Today the millions of visitors pouring through the Park gates only represent an extreme example of man's use of the land, but man's presence there is not new. For centuries man has gone to the Yellowstone to hunt for food, clothing, weapons, and decorative items and precious stones, as well as to seek refuge from hostile groups and climates. It is certainly untrue that aboriginal man avoided the Park because he feared the geysers and hot springs since man-made objects abound near these thermal features. The deep-rutted trails used by Indians to cross the Park to reach the bison-rich plains, remnants of old camps, with their conically stacked tipi poles, and elongated log fences used for directing game drives can still be seen.

How long ago did man first visit Yellowstone Park? Why did he come here and how long did he stay? Who lived here when the first European explorers arrived? What happened to these prehistoric inhabitants? Some answers to these questions can be found in the journals of early trappers, explorers and Park officials or from information gathered through archæological research. In order to understand fully the story of man in Yellowstone, however, it is first essential to consider the setting.

Indians prized obsidian for its lustrous beauty and because it was easily worked and sharpened. This view of Obsidian Cliff and Beaver Lake was photographed by F. Jay Haynes in 1899. (The Haynes Foundation Collection, Montana Historical Society, Helena.)

The Geologic Record

The Yellowstone area consists of a series of high volcanic plateaus averaging over 8000 feet above sea level. These plateaus are composed of massive volcanic flows of welded tuffs, breccias, rhyolite and basalt which are an incredible 3000 feet thick in the vicinity of Yellowstone Lake.[1] About 600,000 years ago volcanic activity took a spectacular turn when a giant caldera (or crater) extending 1000 square miles was formed by a series of violent eruptions in the central region of the Park. Ash and lava were spewed over much of Yellowstone and the Intermountain West. These explosions removed tons of molten rock from just under the earth's surface leaving only the crust, which then collapsed forming the caldera. Subsequent lava flows and forest growth have obscured its gigantic size.

When lava cools quickly, volcanic glass or obsidian is formed. Obsidian is easily worked and sharpened, and it was highly valued by Indians for cutting tools, projectile points and for items of decoration because of its lustrous beauty. Before Columbus, it was an important trade item in Mexico and Guatemala as well as in North America.

The best-known source of obsidian in the Park is Obsidian Cliff located about halfway between Mammoth Hot Spring and Norris Junction in the northwest portion of the Park. Obsidian Cliff is enormous, rising 150 to 200 feet above Obsidian Creek and stretching about a half mile toward the north. The majority of the obsidian available for making stone tools is found near the base of the cliff while the upper portion consists of weathered, porous pumice. This obsidian varies in color from jet black to "dark to light yellowish brown, purplish brown and olive green. . . ."[2] Other sources of obsidian are found in Yellowstone and, as we shall see, were known and used prehistorically.

Of course, the geysers of Yellowstone are the most visible evidence of its volcanic activity, and they continue to mark the presence of tremendous subsurface heat. What we see today in Yellowstone is an array of spouting geysers, bubbling mud, boiling springs and clouds of rising steam and gases. Abundant precipitation provides water for these thermal features that were formed from a combination of geological events. The Park is a spectacle which surely astonished prehistoric people as much as it amazes people today.

In addition to the volcanic disturbances, the face of Yellowstone was further altered by at least three glaciations. Although opinions differ as to times and extent of glaciation, it is generally agreed that the most recent of these, the Pinedale, began about 25,000 years B.C. (before the time of Christ) and persisted until nearly 10,000 B.C. with some ice still clinging to the peaks until 6500 B.C. By this date early hunters were already penetrating the Park and leaving remnants of their stay behind.

Climate

The climate at the end of the last glacial period (usually referred to as the Pleistocene era) was considerably wetter and cooler than it is now. Yellowstone Park was probably very swampy and Yellowstone Lake was at least several feet higher then. As the glaciers gradually melted, this cool, wet period was replaced by a drier, warmer period which lasted from about 7000 to 4500 years ago. It is speculated that during this drier period the south-central portion of the Park may have been free of forests and more amenable to habitation by man. The modern climatic period (since 4500 B.P., before the present) has again been wetter and cooler and has resulted in the dense lodgepole forest which now covers the Park.

For the past 2000 to 3000 years the climate and environment of Yellowstone have been similar to what we see today. The tremendous variety of plant and animal life within the Park is due to the wide range of environments available. A bird's-eye view of the Park reveals that it is surrounded by substantial mountain ranges to the north, east and south. To the west and southwest the Madison and Bechler river systems lead the way into the Madison Valley and the great Snake River Plain. Much of the Park's central portion consists of the Pitchstone, Central, Blacktail and Mirror plateaus. The southern part, characterized by a heavy growth of lodgepole pine gradually opens into broad parks and sage grass meadowlands as one moves north. Complementing these forest and grassland environments are the complex river and lake systems of the Park dominated by magnificent Yellowstone Lake. Many of these waterways are fed by hot water from the thermal springs, which often keeps even the slower portions

F. Jay Haynes photographed elk in the snow in Hayden Valley in the winter of 1894. (The Haynes Foundation Collection, Montana Historical Society, Helena.)

Bison in Yellowstone National Park in the 1800s. Bison were an integral part of the Indian lifeway in prehistoric times. (Photograph by Gifford Photo Archives, Brigham Young University, Provo, Utah.)

of the rivers ice-free year around. Thus, the Park provides a comfortable habitat for many of its wild animals.

Seasonal change, however, is an important characteristic of the Park. Because of its elevation, winters are long in Yellowstone with snow coming almost any time of the year. Temperatures can drop below $-50°$ F. Snowpack accumulates by November and usually persists until May. The snowpack is commonly four to five feet deep on level ground and snowdrifts in the high peaks attain great depths and linger until July or later. Summers are pleasantly cool but brief, lasting from mid-June to late August, and are interrupted regularly by showers. Once the high passes are free of snow and traveling them is fairly easy, they are populated by Rocky Mountain bighorn sheep avoiding the flies that are so bothersome along the rivers.

Animal Life

Game animals, one of the reasons for Yellowstone's continuing attraction, flourish. Prehistoric hunters had available a variety of large grazing animals such as bison, elk, mountain sheep, deer and antelope. Geese, swans and ducks were common on the fish-filled lakes and rivers, while rabbits, squirrels, marmots, ground squirrels, porcupines and several species of grouse were available. In addition to these economically useful species were the predators. Grizzlies and black bears, mountain lions, bobcats, wolves, coyotes and man competed with each other for Yellowstone's resources.

This highly complex, highly diverse system of plants and animals (including man) has maintained a natural balance over thousands of years, even while undergoing constant change. Yellowstone Park has truly provided a special setting for one story of man's encounters with his environment.

2

Prehistoric Man in Yellowstone Park

Just when man first stood in awe of the geysers and mudpots of Yellowstone will probably never be known, but at least 8000 to 10,000 years ago American Indians were visiting the area to hunt for game animals and to seek the highly desirable obsidian found there. Details of the lifestyle of these earliest visitors are difficult to reconstruct, but archæological studies in and near the Park provide glimpses.

In order to understand the fragmented story of prehistoric man in Yellowstone, we must first look at North America as a whole. Scientific research has shown that man arrived on the North American continent at least 12,000 years ago. It is believed that the primary route by which he drifted into the New World was over a broad, 1300-mile-wide land mass called Beringia, now inundated by the shallow waters of the Bering Sea, which was exposed during the late Pleistocene period and which connected northeastern Asia with Alaska. Although cultural remains from this early period are scattered, archæological sites in northeastern Canada, Alaska, Texas, Pennsylvania and elsewhere have been dated to 12,000 B.P. by radiocarbon methods. Some of the earliest, well-defined cultures occur in areas such as the southern Plains, the Great Basin and the Southwest.

Big Game Hunters

Archæological investigations at a number of locations in North America have demonstrated that by 9000 B.C. a distinctive hunting lifestyle had developed east of the Rocky Mountains on the High Plains from Alberta to Texas. This early culture, which is called the Paleo-Indian or Big Game Hunting period, is characterized by the hunting of large mammals including the mammoth, mastodon, the long-horned bison and the horse. These now-extinct animals were killed with spears or darts tipped with distinctive stone projectile points* and thrown with an atlatl or spear-throwing stick. The Great Basin and Plateau areas were also occupied prior to 10,000 years ago, although the lifestyle there appears to have been less focused on hunting.

The earliest Paleo-Indian culture has been labeled "Clovis" after the nearby town in New Mexico where it was first identified. During the period from 9000 to 9500 B.C., Clovis man hunted mammoths (*Mammuthus columbi*) almost to the exclusion of other contemporary large mammals. Mammoth remains, along with the easily recognizable lanceolate (lance-shaped), half-fluted Clovis projectile points are the calling cards of Clovis hunters. Due to changing climatic conditions and perhaps overhunting by man, the mammoth became scarce and the Big Game Hunters concentrated on the long-horned bison (*Bison antiquus*). This was accompanied by a change in the style of projectile points as well. The Folsom point is typical of this period. It is a full-fluted point first identified in New Mexico, smaller than the Clovis point and made by a different technology. Clovis points were finished by a flaking technique called percussion, which involved striking the tool with light blows with a bone, wood or antler baton to shape the point. Folsom points were finished by pressure flaking, which was accomplished by placing the point of the flaking tool exactly where the flake was to be removed and pressing down. This resulted in a more finely finished tool.

The Folsom period spanned about 1000 years, from 8000 B.C. to 9000 B.C. Following this era fluted points go out of style but the hunting of a smaller form of ancient bison, called *Bison occidentalis*, con-

*The term "projectile point" is a generalized label used by archæologists to refer to the chipped stone tools used to tip atlatl darts and spears when the exact function of the tool is not known for sure. Projectile point is usually used in contrast to "arrowhead," which is reserved for reference to the significantly smaller points used on arrows. Arrowheads appear in the archæological record about 2000 years ago.

tinued. This period is referred to as the Plano and is different from the preceding Folsom period in that it is marked by the use of a variety of large, lanceolate projectile points all produced using a highly sophisticated pressure flaking technology. These points are variously called Agate Basin, Hell Gap, Eden, Scottsbluff, Alberta, Angostura, etc., depending on slight differences in size, shape and the geographical area where they were first identified. The age of these points varies and in some cases appears to overlap with the preceding Folsom period. At the end of the Plano period, about 5500 B.C., the Big Game Hunters' way of life begins to change to a rather different, less specialized pattern. Before describing this major change let's examine evidence from the Big Game Hunter period in Yellowstone.

Man apparently visited the Yellowstone area in the Paleo-Indian period between 7500 and 11,500 years ago. In 1959 a portion of a Clovis point was uncovered during the construction of the post office building at Gardiner, Montana, near the north entrance to the Park.[3] Appropriately, the material from which the point was made is obsidian, although it is not known if the obsidian is from the Yellowstone area. A short distance north of Gardiner near Wilsall, Montana, additional evidence of Clovis was found at the Anzick site[4] in the form of a rare Clovis burial with finely made bone points and Clovis-like stone points. East of Yellowstone, the recently excavated Colby site in the Big Horn Basin of Wyoming contained unusual Clovis points in association with mammoth bones.

Although Folsom remains have been found to the north of the Park at the McWaffie site near Helena, Montana, to the southwest in the Snake River Valley of Idaho, and in several sites in Wyoming and southwestern Montana, no recognizable Folsom material has yet been identified in Yellowstone. The following Plano period, however, is fairly well represented in the Park, although all the finds are from the surface. Surface finds are only circumstantial evidence of occupation, and buried deposits dated by radiocarbon analysis or other means are needed to establish the presence of a particular group in an area at a particular time. The dates assumed for these surface artifacts are based on typological cross-dating; that is, even though the early man finds in Yellowstone have not been directly dated, other sites with similar materials have been dated, and those dates can

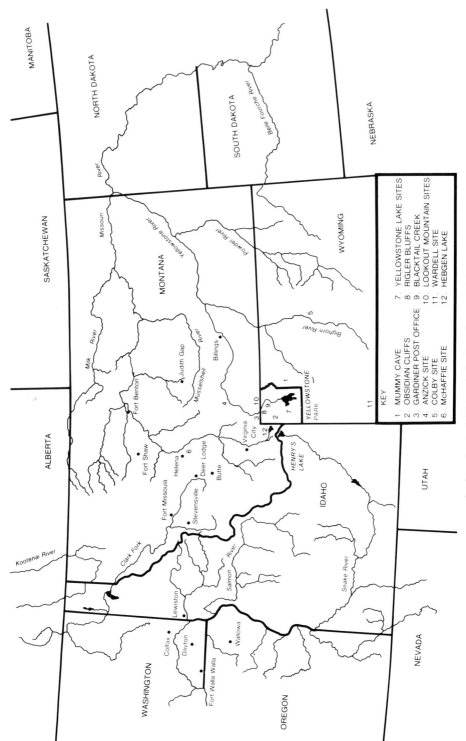

Archaeological Sites of the Northwest Plains

KEY

1 MUMMY CAVE
2 OBSIDIAN CLIFFS
3 GARDINER POST OFFICE
4 ANZICK SITE
5 COLBY SITE
6 McHAFFIE SITE
7 YELLOWSTONE LAKE SITES
8 RIGLER BLUFFS
9 BLACKTAIL CREEK
10 LOOKOUT MOUNTAIN SITES
11 WARDELL SITE
12 HEBGEN LAKE

Mummy Cave with the North Fork of the Shoshone River in the foreground. The cave is located in the center of the photo at the base of the cliff. The two white spots are workers standing in the entrance of the cave. (Jack Richard Studio, Cody, Wyoming, photographer. Print courtesy of Buffalo Bill Historical Center.)

be used for the Yellowstone material with a degree of confidence. Mummy Cave, for instance, immediately east of the Park was occupied sporadically over a 9000-year period.[5] It has been excavated and the various strata dated. Arrow and dart points from dated levels can be compared to surface finds in the vicinity for cross-dating purposes. Basic to this short discussion of dating levels in archæological sites is the cornerstone of archæological dating, stratigraphy or superposition. Simply stated, the concept of superposition assumes that the materials on the bottom in any undisturbed site were laid down first and are therefore the oldest.

Surveys carried out in the Park by archæologists from the University of Montana in Missoula in the late 1950s encountered a variety of Plano material including six Hell Gap points as well as a distinctive tool often associated with Plano period artifacts called a Cody knife.[6] These items were found primarily in the vicinity of Yellowstone Lake but all were within Yellowstone. Immediately to the north of the Park a number of Plano period points are recorded from the Lookout Mountain region. These include Agate Basin, Hell Gap and Eden points. Again all were surface finds and all the points were found on ridges over 9000 feet high, demonstrating that early hunters did not restrict their travels to the lower plains where the bison were found but ventured into many environmental zones. Additional Plano-period materials have been found to the west of the Park along the lower reaches of Grayling Creek and on the north shore of Hebgen Lake.

In addition to this Plano material, which suggests parallels to the Plains groups at that time, several Cascade points were found. These spear or dart points date to approximately the same period as the Plano but are generally found west of the Rocky Mountains in Washington, Oregon and Idaho and indicate some contact with these areas. Because of its geographic location, Yellowstone received visitors and influences from both east and west throughout its history.

The majority of the points mentioned here are made of obsidian that may have been quarried in Yellowstone, although without proper analysis this is speculation. However, the archæological evidence available clearly suggests that the Yellowstone vicinity and the Park itself were visited prior to 7500 years ago by Big Game Hunters who came perhaps to hunt, to obtain obsidian or merely to pass through.

CHRONOLOGY
OF THE
NORTHERN INTERMOUNTAIN REGION

ARCHAEOLOGICAL PERIOD	YEARS	PROJECTILE POINT STYLES	IMPORTANT LARGE ANIMALS	COMMENTS
LATE PREHISTORIC				• Arrival of the horse on the Northern Plains • Pottery appears in Mummy Cave • Anasazi abandon the Four Corners Area
	1000			• Collapse of the Mayan Civilization • Yellowstone obsidian being traded to Ohio
	A.D. 0 B.C.			• The bow and arrow appears in western North America • The beginnings of agriculture north of Mexico
	1000			• Olmec civilization flourishes in Mexico
	2000			
A R C H A I C	3000		Bighorn Sheep Throughout Mummy Cave	• First appearance of pottery in the New World • Pyramids constructed in Egypt
	4000			• Periods of drought on the Plains
	5000			• Corn and other plants domesticated in Mexico
	6000			
	7000			• Modern forms of bison appear • Climate drier and warmer in North America • Mummy Cave first occupied by Man • Plano style projectile points appear
	8000			
PALEO-INDIAN	9000			• Folsom projectile points used to hunt big-horned bison • Climate cooler and more moist than today • Clovis projectile points used to hunt mammoth and mastodon • First solid evidence for the arrival of Man in the New World
	10,000			

Archaic

With the gradual change from the cooler and wetter period of the early post-Pleistocene to the warmer and drier climate we know today, the herds of giant bison, mammoth, horse, camel and other large mammals became extinct. The specialized human lifeway which depended on them was replaced by a broader economic pattern of exploitation known generally throughout North America as the Archaic period. This time is characterized by a greater reliance on gathering plant foods, especially small seeds, and increased hunting of a wider variety of smaller animals, although the modern large animals, such as deer, mountain sheep and bison, continued to be important.

These resources were hunted and gathered during a carefully scheduled yearly round, a system which took shape over hundreds, even thousands, of years. The yearly round was based on the season of the year when particular plants and animals were best gathered or hunted. For instance, fish are most efficiently captured when they are concentrated in their spawning runs, seeds when they are ripe in the greatest numbers, rabbits when they are the fattest, etc. As a result, the movements of the people assumed a definite, predictable pattern based on timely utilization of available resources. The standard tools of these Archaic hunters and gatherers were baskets for collecting seeds and nuts, stone-grinding implements for processing them, and atlatl and snares for hunting. The appearance of these artifacts and associated refuse indicates the wide range of plants and animals utilized and marks the onset of the Archaic period.

This more generalized lifestyle is well documented in Yellowstone, which hosted substantial use during this period. The reason for an increased population may in large part be climatic. The High Plains to the east were plagued with droughts and were not the favorable areas for habitation they had been during the Big Game Hunting period. As a consequence, certain regions, such as the Black Hills and the Rocky Mountains, including Yellowstone, may have been areas with dependable food and water supplies and were therefore more attractive to man. In Yellowstone, Archaic period sites are recognized by large, notched projectile points. These are usually associated with Archaic levels that first appear about 7000 years ago in dated sites such as Mummy Cave. The Yellowstone River valley from the mouth of the Gardner River down to Yankee Jim Canyon contains a number of sites believed to have been used as winter camps during this period. The Rigler Bluffs site near Corwin Springs contained an ancient fire hearth which was dated to 2950 B.C. by radiocarbon methods.[7] Wood recovered from the hearth was identified as western yew, a moisture-loving tree not now found in the area. This hints that the Yellowstone River valley may have received more precipitation then than it does now. The presence of the yew wood, however, was explained in part by geological studies of the setting of the Rigler Bluff site. The hearth was located well away from and above the river, a fact that at first puzzled the scientists. However, by closely analyzing the sediments above and below the hearth, the geologists concluded that about 5000 years ago the Yellowstone River had been blocked by a massive landslide not unlike the one which dammed-up the Madison River in 1959 and formed a lake. The hearth was situated along the edge of such a lake.

Additional concentrations of Archaic sites are reported on the West Gallatin River, in the Clark Fork River valley, the north fork of the Shoshone River and the Corey Springs area on the northeast shore of present Hebgen Lake.

Late Prehistoric

The Archaic lifestyle persisted in some parts of North America until the time of European contact; however, shortly after the time of Christ, changes did occur which affected the eastern Great Basin to the south and, to a certain extent, Yellowstone. These changes are generally viewed as marking the end of the Archaic and the beginning of a more settled lifeway in much of North America. These changes include the adoption of horticulture, or the planting of crops, the development of the bow and arrow, the introduction of pottery, and the development of more substantial houses. Horticulture and pottery were not important in the Yellowstone area but great changes occurred to the south and east at this time because of horticulture; these included increasing sedentism (or settled lifestyles) and a more complex organization of society.

In the great hardwood forests east of the Mississippi River, for example, a complex religion not well understood by scholars resulted in the construction of a large number of burial mounds between 500 B.C. and A.D. 800. They were filled with the bones o the dead and grave offerings. Many of these mounds were of great ize and were built in the shape of animals and geometric forms. The mounds are now assigned to the Adena/Hopewell period by archæologists. They were a source of amazement and entertainment for eighteenth- and nineteenth-century antiquarians who dug for relics and destroyed many of the mounds before research-oriented archæology was attempted.[8]

Among the many grave goods recovered were items foreign to the regions where the mounds were built. These exotic items included conch shells from the Gulf of Mexico, elaborately carved pieces of mica from the southeast, grizzly bear claws from the western plains, and obsidian tools (including flakes and blades, large spears, knives, eccentric objects and projectile points). These tools were long suspected to be from Yellowstone. Obsidian artifacts from 30 sites in Ohio, Illinois, Indiana, Michigan and Ontario were recently analyzed by scientists who successfully demonstrated that the obsidian used by these Hopewellian peoples was quarried over 1500 miles to the west in Yellowstone Park at Obsidian Cliffs and at one other source in the Park.[9] It is not known if the obsidian was obtained by Hopewell traders who traveled from the east to Yellowstone in person or if it was traded from hand to hand until it finally reached the Hopewell region. Archæological research in the region intermediate between the Park and the Midwest has identified Yellowstone obsidian in Iowa, North Dakota and Oklahoma.[10] These findings suggest that obsidian was probably being traded from village to village during prehistoric times.

Although agricultural pursuits were not important in the Yellowstone area, the bow and arrow, which was more powerful, more accurate and more easily manipulated than the atlatl, was adopted by the Plains and Great Basin Indians who traveled through the Park. This transition is marked archæologically by the appearance of smaller, finer projectile points now properly called arrowheads. In dry sites like Mummy Cave the change is also visible through the appearance of bow and arrow fragments.

Blades of Yellowstone obsidian from Hopewell Mounds in Ohio. (Field Museum of Natural History, W. K. Moorehead, 1922.)

Cooperative hunting of large herds of bison had a tradition dating to late Folsom times, but communal drives of these large mammals became more common on the northwestern Plains during the Late Prehistoric period. The earliest known bison drive in which the bow and arrow was used in the area is the Wardell site near Big Piney, Wyoming, dated to about A.D. 500.[11] The Wardell site also contains another new and important item of material culture, pottery. Pottery is useful to archæologists since it preserves well and can be used as a time-marker because of observable changes in form, construction technique and decoration. The pottery at the Wardell site consisted of sherds from a plainware jar with a pointed bottom, a style unlike the flat-bottomed Intermountain pottery which appears perhaps as much as a thousand years later, probably coinciding with the arrival of the Shoshone (see Historic Period). Intermountain pots are usually made in the shape of wide-mouthed jars with a flat, flanged base. Pottery appears quite late in the immediate vicinity of Yellowstone.

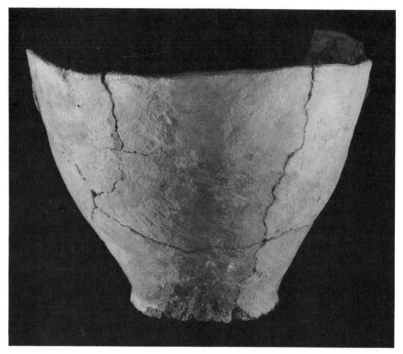

Intermountain pottery from southern Wyoming. (George C. Frison, Prehistoric Hunters of the High Plains, *Academic Press, 1978.)*

At Mummy Cave in 30 feet of deposits only the top 15 or 20 inches contain pottery.

Intermountain pottery was also recovered from buried deposits at a site in the Park near West Thumb Bay on Yellowstone Lake.[12] Additional ceramic finds include sherds from Blacktail Creek, which appear to have been left by groups from farther east—perhaps the Crow Indians. Vessels nearly identical in form to the flat-bottomed pots, but smaller and hewn from a soft stone called steatite, are also reported from the Park. A number of these intriguing vessels have been found in and around Yellowstone but none are dated and their makers are still not clearly identified.[13] Sources of steatite are known in the Big Horn, Wind River and Teton mountains of Wyoming.

The Late Prehistoric period in Yellowstone is a time of heavy occupation compared to the preceding periods. The Yellowstone

Carved steatite vessel from Wyoming. (George C. Frison, Prehistoric Hunters of the High Plains, *Academic Press, 1978.)*

River valley at the north end of the Park is littered with sites from this era. Isolated summer camps are found throughout the Plateau Region as well. Wickiups, stone blinds and log alignments for hunting big-horn sheep and other large game are primarily relics of this period which immediately precedes the arrival of the Euro-American.

3

The Historic Period

The arrival of European explorers in the thirteenth century, and later European settlers, technology, diseases, and social, political and religious systems, mark the Historic period in North America. All of these were new to the Indians of the Americas, and the changes brought to their ancient lifeways were profound and, almost without exception, disastrous.

One introduction which completely changed the lifestyle of many of the Indians of the Intermountain West was the horse. The large conical tipi, flowing feathered headdresses and the importance of war, wealth and status were all encouraged and elaborated with the arrival of the horse. Prior to A.D. 1600, several of the Plains Indians groups —the Sioux, Cheyenne, Crow and others—were farmers living in villages well to the east. The horse changed all of that within a few years by providing a new means of transportation and a more efficient method of hunting bison.

The horse was introduced far to the south of Yellowstone in Santa Fe, New Mexico, where the Spaniards had brought horses in considerable numbers by 1600. From there the horse rapidly spread north and east to the Plains and Plateau regions of western North America, reaching the Shoshone on the plains of Wyoming and eastern Idaho by 1700–20.[14] The horse had a tremendous impact on the lifestyle of the Shoshone as well as on all Indians who chose to use it. As long as there were grasslands to feed the animals, mounted groups could move quickly over long distances while pursuing bison or their enemies. They could now take their families on these trips more easily, carry more baggage, and live in greater comfort. Only the Intermountain and western Plains tribes adopted the horse and developed the nomadic Plains lifestyle (characterized by tipis, pursuit of bison and warrior societies), which constitutes the classic Plains Culture glamorized in western movies and literature.

Those who obtained horses first had their enemies at their mercy. For example, the Shoshone of the northeastern Great Basin and southwestern Wyoming, who obtained horses by 1720, were about 10 to 20 years ahead of their traditional foes the Blackfeet. Mounted and armed with iron trade weapons, the Shoshone expanded as far north as Saskatchewan, pushing their enemies before them. This success was short lived, however. The Blackfeet, armed with guns obtained from British and French traders at Hudson's Bay forced the Shoshone back into their historic homelands in Wyoming and Idaho during the last quarter of the eighteenth century.

Nearly all of the tribes in the Yellowstone region eventually adopted the horse, including groups who lived primarily west of the Continental Divide—the Flathead, Nez Perce, Kalispel, Coeur d'Alene and Shoshone-Bannock. Many of these tribes made annual treks to the Montana and Wyoming prairies to hunt bison on horseback. The Blackfeet, Crow and Eastern or Wind River Shoshone were tribes in the Yellowstone area who lived on the Plains and who also adopted the horse and became part of the Plains Culture. Individuals from all of the groups on both sides of the Divide commonly traveled through or camped in Yellowstone; however, the tribes most frequently mentioned as being in the area are the Blackfeet, Crow and, most importantly, the Shoshone-Bannock.

At the time of Lewis and Clark's historic trip up the Missouri, the Blackfeet controlled the region north of the Park, although they ranged as far south as Idaho and northern Utah at times. The Crow lived to the northeast and east along and south of the Yellowstone River, while various Shoshone speakers* occupied the country to the west, south and southeast of Yellowstone. Also to the west in the upper Snake River Valley region were the Bannock, an enclave of

*The use of the term "speakers" is the first in a number of references in the text to linguistic relationships between Indian groups. Through the study of languages anthropologists can determine which groups of peoples are related and make estimates about how long ago related groups diverged.

Northern Paiute speakers who lived side-by-side with their linguistic cousins the Shoshone. Living within Yellowstone Park and adjacent to mountainous areas were groups of Shoshone speakers named the Sheepeaters after the bighorn sheep which were important game animals to these and other Park hunters. The Sheepeaters are considered to be the primary Indian occupants of Yellowstone during the Historic period.

The boundaries separating these groups certainly were not absolute and all crossed or stayed in the Park at various times. For example, the Wind River Shoshone, also called Washakie's Band, often spent their summers in the vicinity of Yellowstone where they quarried steatite and obsidian, camped and fished around Yellowstone Lake and traded with the Sheepeaters. They also used the waters of the hot springs and pools for religious and medicinal purposes. Although the Sheepeaters were the people who called the Park their home during the nineteenth century, it is important to discuss the Blackfeet and the Crow and give some background on the Shoshone-Bannock, to whom the Sheepeaters were closely related.

Blackfeet

The Blackfeet Indians speak Algonkian, a language related to languages of a number of tribes of central and eastern Canada. The linguistic relationships are relatively distant, however, suggesting a fairly early separation from other Algonkian speakers. Unlike the Cheyenne, Crow and some other Plains groups, the Blackfeet had lived on the northwestern Plains for a long time prior to the arrival of the horse.[15] The Blackfeet were further divided into three loosely affiliated, interacting groups: (1) the *Pikuni* or Piegan, (2) the Kainah or Blood and (3) the Blackfeet. The term Blackfeet is a fairly literal translation of the Algonkian name *Siksikau* (black-footed people).

The Blackfeet were notorious for their warlike attitude and during the 1700s and 1800s were the undisputed rulers of the plains of central Montana and southern Alberta. For example, in 1806 Meriwether Lewis, during his return from the Pacific on the historic Lewis and Clark Expedition, split with Clark and turned north to learn more

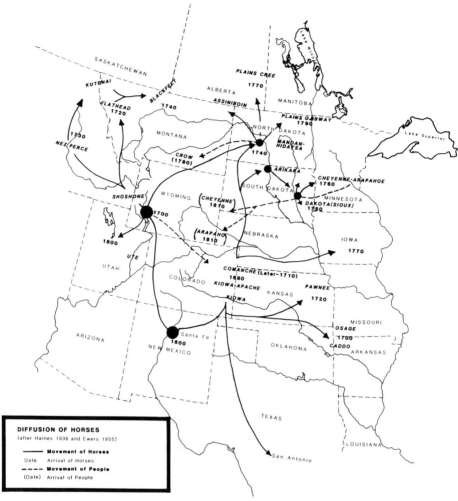

DIFFUSION OF HORSES
(after Haines 1938 and Ewers 1955)

——— **Movement of Horses**
Date   Arrival of Horses
-- -- -- **Movement of People**
(Date) Arrival of People

about the headwaters of the Marias River in northern Montana. While in the area he encountered and was forced by circumstances to camp with a band of Piegan Indians. During the night, the Indians attempted to disarm Lewis and his men and then, failing the former, tried to steal their horses. The ensuing skirmish ended luckily for Lewis's party, despite being outnumbered two to one. They were able to escape with their lives, property and even some of the property of the Indians.[16] Blackfeet numbers were reduced drastically in the early 1800s, and by the time Montana was settled, they were no longer much of a threat.

The presence of the Blackfeet in Yellowstone is heavily documented in the journals of early trappers like Jim Bridger, Daniel Potts,

W. A. Ferris and Osbourne Russell. Russell's journal tells of a number of encounters with Blackfeet in Jackson Hole, on the Madison River near present-day Ennis, Montana, and inside the Park at Pelican Creek on the north side of Yellowstone Lake. This last encounter, which occurred in August of 1839, is described by Russell as follows (the spelling is Russell's):

We were encamped about a half a mile from the Lake on a stream running into it in a S.W. direction thro. a prarie bottom about a quarter of a mile wide   On each side of this valley arose a bench of land about 20 ft high running paralell with the stream and covered with pines   On this bench we were encamped on the SE side of the stream   The pines immediately behind us was thickly intermingled with logs and fallen trees—After eating a few [minutes] I arose and kindled a fire filled my tobacco pipe and sat down to smoke   My comrade whose name was White was still sleeping. Presently I cast my eyes towards the horses which were feeding in the Valley and discovered the heads of some Indians who were gliding round under the bench within 30 steps of me I jumped to my rifle and aroused White and looking towards my powder horn and bullet pouch it was already in the hands of an Indian and we were completely surrounded   We cocked our rifles and started thro. their ranks into the woods which seemed to be completely filled with Blackfeet who rent the air with their horrid yells. on presenting our rifles they opened a space about 20 ft. wide thro. which we plunged   about the fourth jump an arrow struck White on the right hip joint   I hastily told him to pull it out and as I spoke another arrow struck me in the same place but they did not retard our progress   At length another arrow striking thro. my right leg above the knee benumbed the flesh so that I fell with my breast across a log. The Indian who shot me was within 8 ft and made a Spring towards me with his uplifted battle axe: I made a leap and avoided the blow and kept hopping from log to log thro. a shower of arrows which flew around us like hail, lodging in the pines and logs. After we had passed them about 10 paces we wheeled about and took [aim] at them   They then began to dodge behind the trees and shoot their guns   we then ran and hopped about 50 yards further in the logs and bushes and made a stand—I was very faint from the loss of blood and we set down among the logs determined to kill the two foremost when they came up and then die like men   we rested our rifles accross a log

White aiming at the foremost and Myself at the second   I whispered to him that when they turned their eyes toward us to pull trigger. About 20 of them passed by us within 15 feet without casting a glance towards us   another file came round on the [opposite] side with 20 or 30 paces closing with the first a few rods beyond us and all turning to the right   the next minute [they] were out of our sight among the bushes   They were all well armed with fusees [a cheap trade rifle], bows & battle axes.[17]

Russell and his companion were not discovered and, after enduring considerable pain from their wounds and additional hardship, they eventually made their way to Fort Hall in southeastern Idaho.

By 1870, the Blackfeet had suffered a severe population decline due to European introduced diseases, especially smallpox. Major epidemics occurred in 1781, 1837 and 1869–70. Some notion of the seriousness of the decline is suggested by the numbers of Blackfeet dying from smallpox. It is estimated that 6000 Blackfeet, or two-thirds of the entire population, succumbed in the 1837 epidemic alone.[18] In January of 1870, the Blackfeet were further demoralized by the Baker Massacre on the Marias River in which 173 Piegan Indians were killed and a large number were captured. This tragic event marked the end of Blackfeet hostilities. Since 1870, most Blackfeet have lived on reservations in northern Montana and southern Alberta, Canada.

Crow

The Crow Indians were recent arrivals in their territory along the Yellowstone River. According to early accounts, the Crow separated from the Hidatsa farming villages located on the Missouri River in North Dakota about 1776 and arrived in southern Montana shortly after. Horses were undoubtedly acquired prior to the move, and by the time they settled in southern Montana, the Crow were well established in the Plains lifestyle.[19] The Crow, like the Hidatsa, spoke a Siouan* language and their name for themselves, *Ap sar roo kai,*

---

*Siouan is the term used by linguists to refer to a group of related Indian languages spoken by such groups as the Dakota or Sioux tribes (e.g., Teton, Yankton, Sisseton), Mandan, Assiniboine, Osage and Omaha, to name a few besides the Crow and Hidatsa.

actually refers to anything that flies.[20] The Crow were known for flamboyant horsemanship and their beautiful and distinctive styles of decorating clothing and other accoutrements with beads and porcupine quills.

The Crow occasionally traveled through the Park on hunting or raiding excursions. In 1870, for example, the Langford-Washburn party on a historic visit to Yellowstone encountered a group of 100 Crow Indians near Bottler Ranch on the Yellowstone River in the northern portion of the Park. Lt. Gustavus Doane, who provided military protection for the Langford-Washburn group, later lived with the Crow Indians on the Big Horn River of southern Montana and commanded a group of Crow scouts.[21] Although hostilities occurred, these Indians were known generally for their friendship and often served as scouts for the army. The Crow Indian reservation is near this homeland on the Yellowstone River in southern Montana.

Shoshone-Bannock

The people who most often lived in and visited Yellowstone were the Shoshone of southern Idaho, western Wyoming and northwestern Utah and the Bannock, who lived among the Shoshone of southeastern Idaho and who are closely related to the Shoshone.

It is currently believed that the arrival of the Shoshone in this region occurred fairly recently, probably after A.D. 1300. The Shoshone, along with the Northern Paiute to the west and the Ute and Southern Paiute to the south and east, are Uto-Aztecan speakers who, within the last 1000 years, gradually expanded north and east across the Great Basin. This conclusion is based on linguistic as well as archæological studies by scientists working in the Great Basin.[22] These people all spoke a similar language and, for the most part, made their living hunting and gathering wild foods. The Uto-Aztecan linguistic family is a large one, and the language of the Shoshone is related to that spoken by the Hopi of northern Arizona and the Aztec of the Valley of Mexico.

The principal Shoshone groups near Yellowstone were the Lemhi Shoshone, who lived in central Idaho's Lemhi Valley and Salmon River Mountains north of the Snake River Plain, the Northern Sho-

Bannock Indians near the Snake River Agency, Idaho, in the late 1800s. (W. H. Jackson, photographer, Photo Archives, Brigham Young University, Provo, Utah.)

shone of southern Idaho and northern Utah and the Eastern Shoshone of western Wyoming. All the Shoshone were generally referred to by Europeans and neighboring tribes alike as Snakes, a term of uncertain origin.[23] The arrival of the horse in the 1700s served to further differentiate the groups: those who had access to grasslands to support horse herds became equestrian hunters who eventually followed the buffalo to the Plains; those who were not mounted were often referred to as Diggers, a term applied to other Great Basin Indians as well.

The Shoshone tradition for referring to themselves was to name individual groups after a particular food that was important to the livelihood of that group and which was common in the area where they lived. For example, the Shoshone living on the Plains where bison were abundant were called *Kutzundika* or Buffalo Eaters, while those living along the salmon-rich Snake River drainage were referred to as *Agaidika*, Salmon Eaters.[24] Others were called Rabbit Eaters, Pine Nut Eaters, and, of course, the Sheepeaters.

The Bannock were an enclave of Northern Paiute who most likely migrated to southern Idaho in the 1600s or 1700s. The Northern Paiutes closest to the Bannock at the time of European contact were 200 miles to the west in Oregon. The reasons for the presence of a group of Northern Paiute among the Northern Shoshone are not known, but may have been a result of the Bannock moving eastward as the bison diminished in number in the northwestern Great Basin. Regardless, when the first explorers entered Idaho, the Bannock were in place and they remain there today mixed with the Shoshone on the Fort Hall reservation.

The etymology of the term Bannock is, like Snake, difficult to trace. The name Bannock is most likely derived from the Bannock's name for themselves, *Banakwut* or, as the Fort Hall Shoshone referred to them, *Ba naite*. The latter translates as "people from below."[25] Perhaps of most importance is that, despite the linguistic differences, the Bannock and the Northern Shoshone of southern Idaho got along well together. They intermarried, traveled together and were usually bilingual, speaking both Bannock and Shoshone. The language of the Bannock, however, has slowly given way to Shoshone, primarily because of the greater numbers of the Shoshone.[26] Both had adopted the horse by the early 1700s and were committed to the Plains way of life. Buffalo, however, were never as plentiful west of the Rockies as they were on the vast prairies to the east, and treks over the mountains were necessary after about 1840 as the herds on the Snake River Plains were exterminated. These trips often took them through Yellowstone.

Even after the adoption of the horse the Shoshone-Bannock continued to follow many of their old patterns. Winters were spent along the Snake River near Fort Hall between present-day Pocatello and Blackfoot. In the spring and into the summer they traveled west down the Snake to Shoshone Falls, which was the farthest salmon could travel up the river, and to Camas Prairie. Both salmon and camas were obtained on these trips through trade with other Shoshone groups and by gathering the foods themselves. In the later summer the treks to the buffalo country began. Routes taken include the Bannock Trail through Targhee Pass and Yellowstone Park; over Rea's Pass down the Madison River to the Three Forks of the Missouri in Montana; and south of the Yellowstone-Grand Teton region into southwestern Wyoming where they joined with the Wind River Shoshone. The Lemhi Shoshone usually traveled over the Lemhi Pass beyond Virginia City and Bozeman to get to the buffalo grounds.

Many spent the winter in Montana where the climate was sometimes milder than in the Snake River area and where they could hunt for a few weeks in the spring. Others returned to Idaho in the fall and lived on the buffalo meat obtained in Montana and on other stores gathered during the year. This pattern of long-range movement practiced by the horse-riding Shoshone was quite different from the lifestyle of the Sheepeaters of the Salmon River and Yellowstone country.

4

The Sheepeaters

The Shoshone who became known as Sheepeaters lived in the high mountain plateaus and valleys found in Yellowstone Park, the Wind River Mountains of Wyoming and the Lemhi Fork of the Salmon River in central Idaho. Although these mountain dwellers were all called Sheepeaters, they were united only by their pursuit of the bighorn sheep.

The Shoshone term for Sheepeater was *tukaduka* or *tukarika* meaning literally "sheep" (tuka) "eater" (rika).[27] The Sheepeaters of Yellowstone were also referred to as *toyani* or "mountain dwellers" by other Shoshone groups.[28] Some scholars have suggested that *toyani* refers to groups who lived solely in the mountains while *tukarika* refers to more migratory groups.

Sheepeaters probably arrived in the Yellowstone Park area quite recently, perhaps as late as A.D. 1800.[29] Like the other Shoshone of Idaho, the Sheepeaters were part of the slow northeastern migration of peoples across the Great Basin. Their arrival in Yellowstone and neighboring mountain regions marked the maximum permanent movement of the Shoshone north and east.

Early Impressions

The earliest reports of Sheepeaters are from the explorers and trappers who penetrated the Rocky Mountains in the early 1800s. In 1811 the

Hunt party bound for Astoria, Oregon, crossed the Rockies just south of the Grand Tetons and camped near the present town of St. Anthony, Idaho. A Shoshone Indian and his son visited the camp and are described in typical ethnocentric fashion:

> On the 14th day (of October), a poor; half-naked Snake Indian, one of that forlorn caste called the Shuckers, or Diggers, made his appearance at the camp. He came from some lurking-place among the rocks and cliffs, and presented a picture of that famishing wretchedness to which these lonely fugitives among the mountains are sometimes reduced.[30]

About 25 years later, in 1835, Captain Benjamin Bonneville crossed the Wind River Mountains of Wyoming and encountered three Sheepeaters who were described in a similar tone:

> Captain Bonneville at once concluded that these belonged to a kind of hermit race, scanty in number, that inhabit the highest and most inaccessible fastness. They speak the Shoshone language and probably are offsets from that tribe, though they have peculiarities of their own, which distinguish them from all other Indians. They are miserably poor, own no horses, and are destitute of every convenience to be derived from an intercourse with the whites. Their weapons are bows and stone pointed arrows, with which they hunt the deer, the elk and the mountain sheep. They are to be found scattered about the countries of the Shoshones, Flathead, Crow and Blackfeet tribes, but their residences are always in lonely places and the clefts of rocks.[31]

Bonneville's account is balanced by a more informative description found in the journal of the literate and highly active trapper Osbourne Russell. Russell encountered a group of Sheepeaters in the Lamar River Valley of the Park in 1835.

> Here we found a few Snake Indians comprising six men, seven women and eight or ten children who were the only inhabitants of this lonely and secluded spot. They were all neatly clothed in dressed deer and sheepskins of the best quality and seemed to be perfectly happy. They were rather surprised at our approach and retreated to the heights where they might have a view of us without apprehending any danger, but having persuaded them of our

Family group of the Sheepeater band encamped near the head of Medicine Lodge Creek, Idaho, in 1871. (W. H. Jackson, photographer, Bureau of American Ethnology, Smithsonian Institution.)

pacific intentions we succeeded in getting them to encamp with us. Their personal property consisted of one old butcher knife, nearly worn to the back, two shattered fusees which had long since become useless for want of ammunition, a small stone pot and about 30 dogs on which they carried their skins, clothing, provisions, etc. on their hunting excursions. They were well armed with bows and arrows pointed with obsidian.[32]

Shortly after the establishment of Yellowstone as a national park, P. W. Norris, the Park's second superintendent, described the natives of the region as follows:

> These sheepeaters were very poor, nearly destitute of horses and firearms, and, until recently, even of steel or iron hatchets, knives, or other weapons or implements. The stumps and the ends of the poles for lodges, wickeups, and coverts for arrow-shooting, from having been cut by their rude obsidian or volcanic-glass axes, appear not unlike beaver-gnawings. . . . On account of this lack of tools they constructed no permanent habitations, but as evidenced by traces of smoke and fire-brands they dwelt in caves and nearly inaccessible niches in the cliffs, or in skin-covered lodges, or in circular upright brush-heaps called wickeups, decaying evidences of which are abundant near the Mammoth Hot springs, the various fire-hole basins, the shores of Yellowstone Lake, the newly explored Hoodoo region, and in nearly all of the sheltered glens and valleys of the Park.[33]

A half-century later the Sheepeaters of Yellowstone Park are described by the Swedish anthropologist Ake Hultkrantz in one of his several research papers on the Shoshone of Wyoming and Idaho:

> These were mixed with Bannock, and were therefore called by the Shoshoni in other quarters *panaiti toyani* (Bannock mountain dwellers). Judging from the available evidence the *tukudika* have comprised partly an old layer of Shoshoni "walkers," who still retained the mode of life from the period before the introduction of the horse, and who established a culture specialized to suit mountain conditions, and partly impoverished Plains Shoshoni who had lost their horses or who had from fear of the powerful Algonkian and Siouan tribes been obliged to abandon the life on the plains.[34]

Still another account is offered by the noted anthropologist Sven Liljeblad: rather than being impoverished, "the mountaineers (sheepeaters) were much better off than other Shoshoni, save the buffalo hunters." They were big game hunters and, according to Liljeblad, were "the most skilled hunters on foot of all Idaho Indians. . . ."[35]

Among these several descriptions is a common thread that describes the Sheepeater way of life during the period just prior to European contact. The following sections depict the Sheepeaters' culture by comparing these disparate sources.

Lifeway

During the century or so that they inhabited the Yellowstone region, the Sheepeaters lived in the traditional manner of their Great Basin ancestors. The year was divided into a time-proven pattern of movements designed to coincide with the availability of food. This annual round was followed by small camp groups consisting of 2 to 5 families composed of men, women and children in proportions much like what Russell described. Most likely the families were related by blood or marriage. Because horses were a rarity among Sheepeaters, they traveled on foot using dogs as pack animals or carried their belongings on their backs. The use of a dog travois was commonly employed during their moves. The number of camp groups that habitually frequented the Yellowstone Park area is not known for certain, but estimates range from as low as 6 to as many as 15, suggesting that the total Yellowstone Sheepeater population was between 150 and 400. W. H. Jackson, the famous frontier photographer who visited the Park in 1871 with the Hayden expedition, states that there were 340 Sheepeaters "living a retired life in the Mountains dividing Idaho from Montana. . . ."[36] This figure would most likely have included Sheepeaters in Yellowstone and those in the Lemhi River drainage of Idaho.

The social and political organization of the Sheepeaters was simple; each group was led by a headman whose tenure lasted as long as he was able to provide success in hunting and defense against enemies. All individuals in the group were equal in status, making for an egalitarian social structure. Marriage was usually an informal economic union which bound a man and woman together to insure survival. A division of tasks by sex was common in most hunter-gatherer societies. Men hunted, provided defense and did heavy chores and cared for hunting-related tools; women cared for the home, gathered plant foods and prepared the meals. Relatives such as grandparents often lived with the family and assisted in rearing children and doing small chores.

Shoshone encampment at Fort Washakie about 1890. The brush structure on the left resembles the wickiups traditionally made by Great Basin

people and the Sheepeaters. (Photograph by Throsser (?), Photo Archives, Brigham Young University, Provo, Utah.)

The annual round in Yellowstone was related to two seasons, summer and winter. In summer the Shoshones were high in the mountains pursuing the mountain sheep. The meat was preferred by all prehistoric Indians of this region, and the sheepskins were raw materials for clothing and accessories. Horns from the rams were used to make special tools. Summer was also a time for fishing in the streams of Yellowstone and for gathering various greens, roots and berries as they ripened. Birds, like mountain grouse and waterfowl, and many small mammals, including beaver, marmots, ground squirrels, and porcupines, were available in considerable numbers in the summer. The pursuit of these foodstuffs would have occasionally carried the Sheepeaters out of the mountains into lower river valleys, such as the Yellowstone, Madison and Snake or the Henry's Lake region, where they would likely have met the Bannock who often spent time there. Camps during the snow-free period were of short duration since the Indians moved on a tight schedule following the pattern of food availability.

During the winter, camps were semipermanent. The Sheepeaters settled in a sheltered creek or river bottom with convenient access to wood, fresh water and yarding elk, sheep, deer or even bison.

Houses

Sheepeater shelters probably took several forms and followed the pattern of their unmounted Shoshone-speaking cousins of the Great Basin. Foremost among these was the domed willow or brush wickiup, which was constructed by placing a number of small, pliable poles in a circle 10 to 15 feet in diameter, bending them into the center, and tying the tops together to form a sort of hogan or igloo shape. This superstructure was covered with slabs of bark, hides or sheaves of grass that may have been secured with encircling withes of willow tied into place. A hole was left in the center of the roof to let smoke escape and a doorway was placed on the side away from the prevailing wind. In winter, reinforcements of logs, stones and earth were piled around the perimeter for protection from the cold. Usually two families called these wickiups their home.

War lodge in the northern Bighorn Mountains similar to the wickiups found in Yellowstone. (George C. Frison, Prehistoric Hunters of the High Plains, *Academic Press, 1978.)*

The other important structure was a sort of windbreak made by planting a semicircle of poles in the ground and piling branches against them to break the powerful winds that often blow in the Rocky Mountains. This roofless shelter could be erected quickly by a small group of people and was therefore ideal for use during the summer when camps were moved frequently. Variations on this windbreak and the domed wickiup were sometimes combined with the face of a cliff or rock overhang in order to take advantage of the extra protection and warmth of the stone.

Several conical "wickiups," consisting of up to 100 poles placed in a tipi-like circle, remain in Yellowstone and have been attributed to the Sheepeater. However, these structures were not in the Shoshone tradition; they more closely resemble war lodges erected by the Crows, who occasionally traveled in Yellowstone Park.[37]

Clothing and Crafts

According to Osbourne Russell, the clothing worn by the Sheepeaters consisted of beautifully tanned elk, deer or sheepskins which were used for shirts and leggings. The beauty of these tanned skins was due to using two brains* per hide rather than one, which was the norm for most Indian tannings.[38] Women's dresses were made from two carefully tanned mountain sheep hides. Tough badger and elk skins were made into hunters' moccasins, while soft deerskins were made into more comfortable footwear; fox and coyote skin, with the fur left on, were used for hats and leggings, and tanned antelope skins were lined with rabbit fur to make warm blankets. The most highly prized blankets were of wolfskin, which symbolized both a hunter's skill and the tanner's art. Because of the quality of their tanned skins, Sheepeaters were able to trade them to Plains groups for buffalo robes. Osbourne Russell "obtained a large number of elk, deer and sheep skins from them [Sheepeaters] of the finest quality and three neatly dressed panther skins in return for awls, axes, kettles, tobacco, ammunition, etc."

*Animal brains were rubbed into the hide to soften it during the tanning process. Using two brains rather than one produced a softer, more pliable hide.

The Sheepeaters also excelled at making bows from the horns of various animals. According to Russell, "the bows were beautifully wrought from Sheep, Buffalo and Elk horns secured with Deer and Elk sinews and ornamented with porcupine quills and generally about 3 feet long." These powerful composite bows were made from the thick ridges on the upper side of a mountain sheep ram's horns by heating the horn to make it pliable and then straightening it. Excess horn was trimmed off, and the piece was heated and shaped until a tapered piece 18 to 24 inches long, one inch thick at the butt and oval in cross section remained. An identical piece was fashioned from the opposite horn. The two ends were then carefully beveled and fitted together and joined by laying a short separate piece of horn over the joint. The joint was then tightly wrapped with wet rawhide. The bow was further strengthened by glueing strips of animal sinew to the back. Such a bow took two months to make and could drive an arrow completely through a buffalo. Small wonder that the bows were highly prized by the Sheepeaters and other Shoshone groups who would give five to ten ponies for a good one.

Other weapons and tools important to the Sheepeaters were arrows tipped with small sidenotched points, stone knives and scrapers for butchering game and processing the hides and stone pots for cooking. Arrows were sometimes tipped with a poison made from the roots of local plants to ensure success.[39] Although stone pots were heavy for nomadic people to carry from place to place and were undoubtedly often cached, we do know from Russell's firsthand description that some groups did carry their stone pots with them. These stone pots may be the steatite vessels pictured in Chapter 2 since the shape is very similar to Intermountain pottery probably made by the Shoshone during the last 500 years. Heavily used steatite quarries with caches of vessel blanks* nearby have been found within the traditional territory of the Sheepeaters—the Wind River, Teton and Big Horn ranges of Wyoming.

By 1800, the Sheepeaters did have access to European trade goods including metal for knives, axes, awls and arrow and spear points,

---

*Vessel blanks are large chunks of steatite which have been roughly shaped, but not completely finished into the final vessel form.

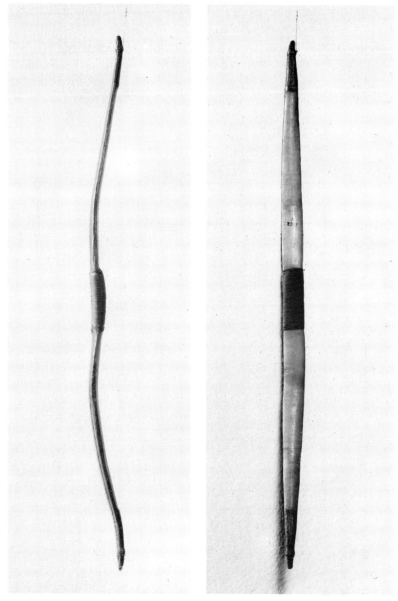

Nez Perce bow of mountain sheep horn. (Neg./Trans. No. 324351, 324352, photography by Rota, courtesy of Department Library Services, American Museum of Natural History, Cat. No. 1/2707.)

glass trade beads, buckets and guns and ammunition. Russell's description makes it clear that these exotic items were available, but only in limited numbers so they probably did not affect their lifestyle. Grinding implements of stone were used by the Sheepeaters for processing plant foods. Seeds and nuts were placed on flat, smoothed stones (metates) and ground with bun-shaped manos into a coarse flour to be used in mushes. Berries, roots and meat were pounded in a stone bowl (a mortar) with an elongate stone called a pestle. Like the steatite pots, these heavy tools were often left at the camps where the processing was done and used during subsequent stops. It is also important to mention digging sticks used to procure roots. They were carefully made from strong elastic woods, such as mountain mahogany or serviceberry, and were sharpened and fire hardened. They were sometimes padded on the upper end and a crosspiece of bone or elk antler affixed to provide a good handle. Well-made digging sticks were prized by the women, who did most of the root gathering.[40]

Food and Food Getting

Sheepeater hunting practices did not rely solely on the use of the bow and arrow. In their pursuit of large game, such as the bighorn sheep, they constructed rather elaborate traps of timber to capture several animals at once. Col. P. W. Norris, the Park's second superintendent, describes them.

> Other traces of this tribe are found in the rude, decaying, and often extensive pole and brush fences for drive-ways of the deer, bison, and other animals, to the narrow-coverts, in the canyons or in the narrow passes between them, for slaughter with the rude lances and obsidian-headed arrows.
>
> For want of proper tools, but little timber was cut, and these drive-ways were mainly constructed of the ever-abundant dead and fallen saplings, with the roots attached, which, from their pitchy properties, long outlast the trunks and branches, thus enabling an experienced mountaineer to trace these drive-ways a long distance, even in groves of thrifty timber. . . . Countless drive-ways and coverts in every state of decay are still found in

Remains of a mountain sheep trap in the Wind River Mountains of Wyoming. (George C. Frison, Prehistoric Hunters of the High Plains, *Academic Press, 1978.)*

favorable localities throughout the Park, and are often crossed unobserved by ordinary tourists.[41]

Similar game traps outside the Park in the Wind River and Absaroka mountains, which have been investigated archæologically, contained mountain sheep bones in the catch pen leaving little doubt as to the intended quarry.[42] Fences over 10 feet high were constructed and had an inward lean to prevent sheep from jumping or clambering over the top.

Hunters also ambushed their prey at known haunts, such as salt or mineral licks, or along narrow saddles where game trails crossed mountain ridges. Dogs were sometimes used to assist in hunting large game. Snowshoes were employed in the winter so the hunter could run quickly over the snow while hoofed animals, such as sheep and elk, would bog down. Elk were occasionally shot at night when the animals visited mineral deposits to "lick the clay."[43]

Fish, especially trout and whitefish, were abundant in certain areas of Yellowstone and were eaten by the Sheepeaters. Fishing was mostly done with spears and snares, especially during the spawning runs in the late spring and early summer. Nets and weirs apparently were not used.[44] Along the edge of Yellowstone Lake, however, there are stone alignments that may have functioned as part of a fish trapping system constructed by peoples who lived in Yellowstone before the Sheepeaters.

Vegetable foods played a major role in the diet of the Sheepeaters. The seasonal ripening of roots, seeds, nuts and berries was probably more important in determining when the Sheepeaters moved to their next camping area than the availability of game. The harvest season was short and careful attention had to be paid to the stage of development of these plants or the seeds, nuts or berries would ripen and drop to be quickly eaten by birds, bears or other animals. Game was less predictable and the timing of hunts was less critical. Berries, such as huckleberries, raspberries, chokecherries, serviceberries and others were picked in season as were various greens, bulbs and roots. Roots were especially important to the prehistoric people of the Great Basin and the people who lived north in Idaho, Oregon and Washington. Yamp, bitterroot, tobacco root and camas were all gathered and eaten in the spring when the roots were new and succulent or later in the fall when they had grown to a greater size. Camas grew in abundance in regions like Camas Prairie in southern Idaho and in other meadowlands such as Henry's Lake flats just west of the Park. These roots were dug with digging sticks and cleaned and baked for several days in earth ovens. They were then eaten or, after pounding and additional cooking and drying, stored for consumption during the cold and often lean winter months. Berries were likewise ground and dried in the form of small cakes and stored. They provided a popular seasoning for otherwise bland mushes made from ground seeds or nuts. Ants and grubs were also on the Sheepeater menu and were generally roasted before eating.

Like the pinyon pine, which produced nuts in abundance for Great Basin Indians, the limber pine produced nuts in quantity for

Indians farther north. Limber nuts were collected and processed by hulling and grinding the meats into a flour that then was mixed with water to make mush.

The history of the Sheepeaters is not well known. Protected by isolation, they resisted for some time the many changes that were affecting surrounding Indian groups. However, incursions of Plains groups into Yellowstone during the nineteenth century caused Sheepeaters to ally more closely with Washakie's band of Wind River Shoshone. This contact resulted in the acquisition of some horses and an amalgamation into fewer and larger bands. Some political unity was achieved during this time under head chief Toyæwowici.

After Yellowstone became a national park in 1872, the presence of Sheepeaters was perceived as a potential deterrent to tourist traffic by Park superintendent Col. P. W. Norris, especially after the Nez Perce campaign of 1877. To insure that Indians stayed out of Yellowstone, Norris lobbied hard in Washington in 1880 for a treaty excluding all Crow, Bannock and Shoshone, including Sheepeaters, from the Park. Upon his return from Washington he visited several reservations to pave the way for the acceptance of these treaties, which were ratified by Congress in 1882. A significant event in the history of the Sheepeaters was the so-called Sheepeater War of 1879 which, although it occurred in central Idaho, certainly affected the Yellowstone group. The affair was precipitated by the killing of five Chinese and two Anglos near Challis, Idaho. Gen. O. O. Howard sent two detachments of soldiers to the Middle Fork of the Salmon where they campaigned for four months. Finally, 51 Indians, including 15 "warriors," were captured. According to Sven Liljeblad, the "armament of this formidable foe, pursued for three months by the United States Cavalry, mounted infantry, and enlisted Umatilla Scouts, totaled four carbines, one breech-loading and two muzzle-loading rifles, and one double-barreled shotgun."[45]

As a consequence of the Sheepeater War and the lobbying by Norris, most of the Sheepeaters of Yellowstone moved either to the Wind River Shoshone Indian reservation in Wyoming or the Fort Hall Shoshone-Bannock reservation near Blackfoot, Idaho. Some probably also went to the Lemhi reservation on the Idaho-Montana border as well. In 1882 a few Sheepeaters returned to their mountain home to guide General Sheridan's exploration of parts of Wyoming,

Idaho and Montana. The most distinguished of these guides was the Sheepeater chief Togwatee, who eventually became an important leader among the Wind River Shoshone.

With the banning of all Indians from the Park, the region soon took on the appearance of an area used only in the distant past. When General Sherman came through in 1877 he wrote, "We saw no signs of Indians. . . ." But as we shall see, the Park soon provided the setting for a portion of one of the most celebrated conflicts between the Indians and the U.S. Army—the Nez Perce War.

5

The Bannock Trail

In the northern portion of Yellowstone Park, between Indian Creek
and the Lamar River, remnants of the Bannock Trail are still clearly
visible to those who know where to look. This trail was named for
the Bannock Indians, who were perhaps its primary travelers. It came
to be an important route for all groups of horse-riding Idaho Indians
who depended heavily on the bison for food, buffalo robes and other
domestic items. Fort Hall and Lemhi Shoshone, Nez Perce and Flathead all used the trail separately and sometimes together.

This route through Yellowstone was likely used throughout much
of prehistory, but it experienced greatly increased travel during the
mid-1800s. The reasons for this are historical. Prior to about 1840
buffalo were relatively abundant in the Snake River Valley, the
northern Great Basin and the Uintah Basin of Utah. In 1841,
Osbourne Russell comments on the drastic change in the availability
of big game in these regions:

> In the year 1836 large bands of buffalo could be seen in almost
> every little valley on the small branches of this stream; at this time
> the only traces which could be seen of them were the scattered
> bones of those that had been killed. Their trails which had been
> made in former years, deeply indented in the earth, were over-
> grown with grass and weeds. The trappers often remarked to each
> other as they rode over these lonely plains that it was time for
> the white man to leave the mountains as beaver and game had
> nearly disappeared.[46]

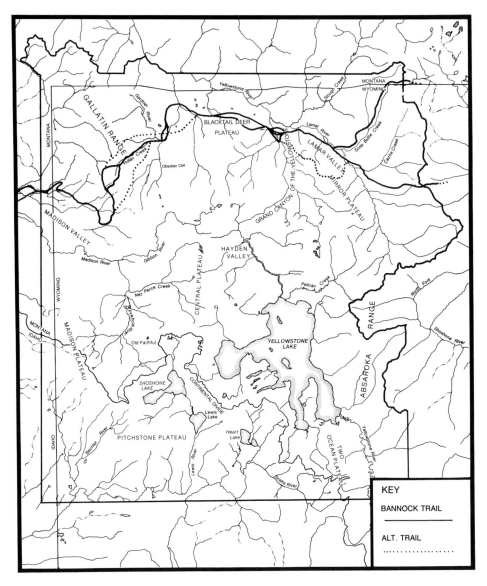

KEY

BANNOCK TRAIL

————

ALT. TRAIL

....

The Great Bannock Trail in Yellowstone Park (after Replogle, 1956).

The blame for the extermination of the buffalo in the Great Basin can probably be placed on the arrival of the horse and firearms. Once the buffalo were gone, Indian groups west of the Rockies who had adapted the Plains lifestyle preferred hunting the bison in Blackfeet and Crow enemy territory to returning to their former lifeway. Warm buffalo robes, spacious tipis and hundreds of pounds of meat were certainly more attractive than the rabbit skin robes, brush wickiups, and seed gathering used a century before.

Early Routes

Undoubtedly the Bannock Trail was only one of many routes used by prehistoric man to move across the Rockies. For example, the easiest route for the Bannock to move from the Pacific to the Atlantic drainage was to simply drop over the barely perceptible continental divide at Raynold's Pass which separates Henry's Lake from the valley of the Madison and the Three Forks area buffalo hunting grounds. Significantly, Three Forks was within territory claimed by the Blackfeet who, as we know, were historical enemies of the Bannock and Shoshone. Relatively easy routes over the mountains also lay to the east and southeast, but these led into ranges already depleted of game by the Eastern Shoshone, the Ute and trappers. The remaining route lay to the north and east across the Park and friendly Sheepeater country and onto the rich hunting grounds of Montana. Part of the appeal of the Bannock Trail was the strategic advantage that it offered. As it cut across the northern portion of the Park, the Trail accessed a series of river valleys that were potential avenues to the buffalo prairies. While the main camp waited in the safety of the mountains, fast-moving scouts could be dispatched down the rivers (for example, the Madison, Gallatin, Yellowstone or Clarks Fork) to check for the presence of enemy camps and locate game.

The trail began to the south and west of the Park near Camas Meadows, ascended Henry's Fork of the Snake River and entered the Yellowstone region via Henry's Lake flats and Targhee Pass. Near Horse Butte, a few miles north of West Yellowstone in the upper Madison Valley, the Bannock Trail was joined by branch trails from the Madison and Gallatin valleys. From here the main trail entered present-day Yellowstone Park along the Duck Creek drainage toward the head of Cougar Creek and then cut north to pass over the Gallatin Range just west of Mount Holmes at an elevation of 9300 feet. The trail then descended Indian Creek to its juncture with Gardner River and turned across Swan Lake flats and over Snow Pass to Mammoth.

Here it was joined by other minor trails coming up the Yellowstone drainage.

The trail stayed generally south of the Yellowstone River as it crossed the Gardner River, Lava Creek and Blacktail Deer Creek. After fording the Yellowstone River near Tower Falls, the trail followed the Lamar River to its juncture with Soda Butte Creek where the trail split, one track following a more circuitous route to the Clarks Fork along Soda Butte Creek, and another leaving the Lamar River and striking directly over the divide and into the Clarks Fork drainage. Assorted side routes and minor trails along with the main trail just described combined to form a system of prehistoric travel through Yellowstone which varied with such factors as the weather, presence of enemy groups and game.

The trail led ultimately to a favorite hunting ground of many of the western tribes including the Nez Perce, Kalispel, Kutenai, Pend d'Oreille, Flathead and Shoshone. This hunting ground lay between the Yellowstone and Musselshell rivers of south-central Montana. The Shoshone called it *Kutsunambihi*, "the buffalo heart," after a heart-shaped rock formation located about 40 miles northwest of Billings, Montana. Apparently the area was intermediate between traditional territories of the Crow and Blackfeet, but was claimed by both. The effect was that the region was somewhat neutral.[47]

The Bannock Trail, 1838–78

As mentioned earlier, the Park had been traversed by man for centuries, but the extermination of the buffalo in the Basin-Plateau region resulted in a surge of traffic along this thoroughfare during a 40-year period between 1838 and 1878. Haines has described the use of the Bannock Trail over the 40-year period in three phases. The first, from 1838 to 1862, were the "golden years" when the Bannock traveled freely to the buffalo grounds. No treaties bound them, no settlers intruded upon their homeland and Yellowstone was still "undiscovered." The second phase lasted from 1862 to 1868. This was a time of transition from the traditional patterns of unfettered movement to the settling on the Fort Hall Reservation. The reservation was formed as a consequence of numerous factors including the

Battle of Bear River where Gen. Patrick E. Connor massacred a large group of Shoshone and some Bannocks. In this period the Bannocks had to reroute the trail southward over the rugged Absaroka Mountains to avoid mines discovered in the Cooke City area. During the third phase, 1868–78, the Bannock were being pressured by the reservation agent to settle down, but without the annual trek to obtain buffalo they were faced with starvation. A critical event at this time was the death of chief Targhee on the prairies east of the Park in the winter of 1870–71. Unfortunately, no comparable chief arose to lead the Bannock. Due to conflicts with the other struggling tribes, the Sioux, Nez Perce, Arapahoe and Crow, and finally skirmishes with settlers, the Bannock were asked to give up their homes and guns— a request that led to the short-lived Bannock War of 1878. The Bannock were returned to the reservation and officially merged with the Shoshone by the Commissioner of Indian Affairs.

The Bannock and Northern Shoshone now make their home near Blackfoot, Idaho, on the Fort Hall reservation. Modern highways through the Park closely follow the Bannock Trail and other prehistoric paths trod for centuries by these Indians.[48]

6

The Nez Perce War

In the spring and early summer of 1877 in the Wallowa Valley of eastern Oregon, a combination of events revolving around the attempts of the U.S. government to place the Nez Perce on a reservation culminated in an outbreak of hostilities between the Indians, the local settlers and the military. After a series of skirmish victories fought against U.S. troops, five of the Nez Perce bands, more or less united under the leadership of a chief named Looking Glass, decided their best chance for freedom lay in a retreat east into Montana where they could either find refuge with the Crows or flee into Canada.

Battle of the Big Hole

About 200 men, 550 women and children and more than 2000 horses fled through the rugged Bitterroot Mountains and crossed over Lolo Pass southwest of Fort Missoula, Montana. After a brief skirmish with troops at "Fort Fizzle"* near Missoula, and perhaps feeling assured of their safety because of the friendly attitude of local whites,

---

*Just above the mouth of Lolo Creek the Nez Perce encountered a crude log barricade hastily constructed across the canyon by a group of enlisted men and civilian volunteers under the direction of Captain Charles C. Rawn of the Seventh Cavalry stationed at Fort Missoula. Backed by his small group of regulars and volunteers, Rawn attempted to detain the Indians, but the Nez Perce simply detoured over the mountain to the north and avoided the obstacle. His feeble barricade was jokingly nicknamed Fort Fizzle by amused locals.

A late nineteenth-century photograph of Gen. Oliver Otis Howard. (Photograph from James A. Taylor's scrapbook, Bureau of American Ethnology, Smithsonian Institution.)

the Nez Perce slowed their retreat. The route they took, at the insistence of Looking Glass, was southerly, much to the consternation of many of the warriors who wanted to quickly turn north and escape to Canada.

Meanwhile, Gen. O. O. Howard, who was in charge of the pursuit of these "renegades," wired Fort Shaw, Montana, for troops to cut off the Nez Perce retreat while he followed their route over the Lolo Trail. The Fort Shaw troops, led by Col. John Gibbon, moved quickly to overtake the Indians and their numbers swelled to over 250 when they were joined by the very settlers who recently befriended the Nez Perce. On the morning of August 9, 1877, these troops and settlers viciously attacked the sleeping village of Nez Perce camped on the Big Hole River near Wisdom, Montana. Even with the element of surprise on his side, Gibbon was unable to defeat the Indians, and sustained heavy casualties (29 dead, 40 wounded). Heavy casualties were also inflicted on the Indians. The battle lasted throughout the hot summer day and by afternoon, Gibbon, who initially thought he would be an easy victor, found himself pinned down as the Nez Perce warriors reversed the advantage. Gibbon was eventually saved by the arrival of Gen. Howard. Between 60 and 90 Nez Perce died at the Battle of the Big Hole, mostly women and children. Twelve of their best warriors were also killed including the important leaders Rainbow and Five Wounds.

Smarting from this loss, the Nez Perce bands fled south along the east slope of the divide under new leadership since Looking Glass, whose attitude had lulled the Indians into a false sense of security, was out of favor. The new leader, Poker Joe, was half-French, half-Nez Perce and knew the Montana trails well. The angry Nez Perce crossed the divide into Idaho at Bannock Pass raiding as they went and met with Tendoy, chief of the Lemhi Shoshone, at the Lemhi reservation near Junction, Idaho. The Shoshone wanted nothing to do with the Nez Perce. In fact, the Shoshone and Bannock at Fort Hall were anxious to do battle. Gen. Howard had employed a contingent of Bannock scouts and allowed them to scalp and mutilate Nez Perce corpses at the Big Hole battleground. Eventually, the Nez Perce were to discover that even their former confederates, the Crow and Cheyenne, had also become their enemies, so fickle were the alliances of Plains warrior groups.

The Flight East

Meanwhile, Howard joined with Gibbon to head off the fleeing Indians by staying on the east side of the divide until he reached Monida Pass. Fearing the Indians would cross the Rockies and escape onto the Plains via the northern Yellowstone route, Howard sent 40 troops on a shortcut through Centennial Valley to cut the Nez Perce off at Targhee Pass just a few miles west of present-day West Yellowstone. Howard and the main body of soldiers, which had now been

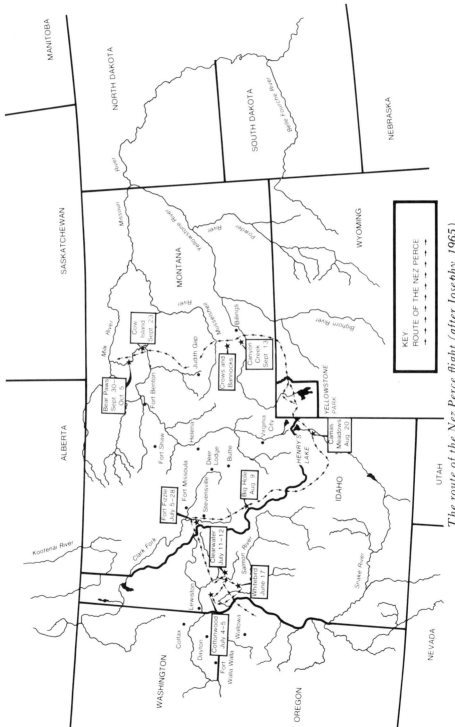

The route of the Nez Perce flight (after Josephy, 1965).

reinforced by 50 cavalry troops from Fort Ellis near Bozeman, Montana, camped at Camas Meadows in Idaho only a day behind the Indians. Here the Nez Perce took the offensive by doubling back and stealing 200 head of mules and generally harassing the army. While this battle was being engaged, the troops at Targhee Pass, who had been unable to locate the Indians, became anxious and, thinking the Nez Perce had gone south through the Tetons, decided to rejoin Howard. Incredibly, these troops not only managed to miss seeing the Indians and their large horse herd, but also managed to miss Howard, who arrived at Henry's Lake and Targhee Pass to find his troops gone and to discover the trail of the Nez Perce heading over the pass into Yellowstone.

By this time the Nez Perce War had become a major news item on the East Coast with the Indians being cast in the role of underdogs and Howard being perceived as a pontifical, bungling general who was continuously outwitted by the brilliant Nez Perce leader, Chief Joseph. Joseph was one of several chiefs and was not a war leader but, because of an initial misunderstanding by Howard at the outset of the war, Joseph had been described as the leader of the hostilities from the beginning. Gen. Sherman pressured Howard to pursue the matter with vigor or give his command to a younger man. Stung by these remarks, Howard assured Sherman that he intended to persevere until the compaign concluded with the defeat of the Nez Perce.

Refreshed after three day's rest and inspired by his exchange with Sherman, Howard again took up the trail. Afraid that the arrival of the group of warlike Nez Perce on the Plains might stir up trouble among the recently subdued Sioux and other Plains groups, the army sent help. Two companies of cavalry under Lt. Gustavus Doane and six companies of Custer's old Seventh Cavalry led by Col. Samuel D. Sturgis were dispatched by Col. Nelson Miles to assist Howard in trapping the Nez Perce in Yellowstone. Doane ascended the Yellowstone River from the north while Sturgis skirted the Park and set up a blockade on the Clarks Fork River where it was expected the Indians would appear. Gen. Sherman had a change of heart and decided to transfer Howard's command to Lt. Col. C. C. Gilbert, then stationed at Fort Ellis. Ironically, Gilbert, bearing his letter of authorization, searched in vain through the Park for Gen. Howard and, failing to find him, finally returned to Fort Ellis.

The Nez Perce War in Yellowstone

The Indian bands, under the direction of Poker Joe and unaware of all the hoopla, had wisely decided against traveling the better-known and longer Bannock Trail. They chose instead a more direct, although a less familiar, route across the Park which took them up the Madison and Firehole rivers. They eventually camped at the juncture of the Firehole and Nez Perce Creek. By 1877 Yellowstone had been a national park for five years and, incongruous as it may seem, there were tourists in the Park.

The Indians first encountered an old prospector named John Shivley camped alone on the Firehole River a mile or so above Nez Perce Creek. While eating supper, Shivley was surrounded and captured by the Indians who pressed him into service as a guide. Believing it would not be wise to refuse and knowing something of the country, he helped lead the Nez Perce through the Park for the next 13 days before finally escaping. Apparently because they were south of the well-known Bannock Trail, the Indians were having a difficult time finding their way.

Shivley later told the tale of his adventure with the Nez Perce to Mr. James H. Mills who recounted it.

There are from 600 to 800 Nez Perces in the band. Of these 250 are warriors but all will fight that can carry a gun. They have almost 2000 head of good average horses. Every lodge drives its own horses in front of it when traveling, each lodge keeping its band separate. The line is thus strung out so that they are three hours getting into camp. They are nearly all armed with repeating rifles, only half a dozen or so having muzzle loaders. They say they have more ammunition than they want. About one-sixth of the horses are disabled, lame or sore-backed, but they keep changing and hold all the good horses in reserve. The horses are all in fair condition. They seemed at first anxious about the soldiers overtaking them but soon got over that, and had no intimation any troops were trying to intercept them in front. They kept no scouts ahead and after crossing the Yellowstone had no rear guard, only a few parties striking out occasionally on their own account.

So far as he could notice no particular chief seemed to be in command. All matters were decided in a council of several chiefs.

Thunder Coming From the Water up Over the Land, *commonly known as Chief Joseph of the Nez Perce. (Charles M. Bell, photographer, Bureau of American Ethnology, Smithsonian Institution.)*

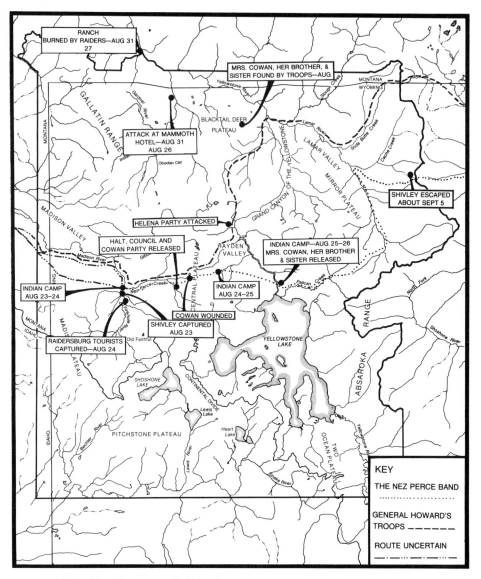

The Nez Perce travels in Yellowstone Park during the war (after Brown, 1966).

White Bird was not known to him at all, as such, but thinks he was present in the councils in about a dozen of which Shivley participated. Joseph is about thirty-five years of age, six feet high, and always in a pleasant mood, greeting him each time with a nod and smile. Looking Glass is 50 or 60 years old. He wears a white feather, and Joe Hale (Poker Joe) two, putting a new feather in his cap after Mr. Shivley joined them. They say they have lost 43 warriors altogether, of these 6 or 7 were killed in Norwood's fight near Camas Meadows, the remainder at Big Hole, where they lost many women and children. Joe Hale says he killed two soldiers there. They had but 10 or 12 wounded with them and one was dying when Shivley escaped. They said they would fight soldiers but did not want to fight citizens—but Mr. S. (Shivley) says they will kill anybody.[49]

Later that same evening Nez Perce scouts discovered the campfire of nine tourists from Radersburg, Montana. The Indians captured the party the following morning to keep them from informing the army and dragged the entire group with them as they traversed the Central Plateau toward Hayden Valley.

The Cowan party, as it came to be known, included Mr. and Mrs. George Cowan, Mrs. Cowan's brother and sister, Frank and Ida Carpenter, J. Albert Oldham, William Dingee, Charles Mann, A. J. Arnold and D. L. Meyers. The tourists were treated relatively well at first, but as the day progressed the younger warriors grew increasingly insolent and began exchanging their worn equipment for the tourists' newer and better saddles, guns and horses. Poker Joe was afraid trouble might break out and warned the members of the group that they should try to escape at the first opportunity. Two points seem clear from this action: first, the chiefs did not wish to harm the tourists; and second, this incident demonstrates the lack of control Plains Indian leaders had over individual members of their following.

Shortly after Poker Joe gave his advice two of the tourists, Dingee and Arnold, escaped. As a result some of the younger warriors lost their tempers and shot George Cowan first in the leg and then in the head, apparently killing him. Cowan was left where he lay while his wife fainted and, with her hysterical sister, was dragged on to the Yellowstone River. She and the others were eventually released. Mrs. Cowan published the story of the ordeal in several periodicals and described the moment when her husband was shot.

Suddenly, without warning, shots rang out. Two Indians came dashing down the trail in front of us. My husband was getting off his horse. I wondered for what reason. I soon knew, for he fell as soon as he reached the ground—fell headlong down the hill. Shots followed and Indian yells, and all was confusion. In less time that it takes me to tell it, I was off my horse and by my husband's side, where he lay against a fallen pine tree. I heard my sister's screams and called to her. She came and crouched by me, as I knelt by his side. I saw he was wounded in the leg above the knee, and by the way the blood spurted out I feared an artery had been severed. He asked for water, I dared not leave him to get it, even had it been near. I think we both glanced up the hill at the same moment, for he said, "Keep quiet. It won't last long." That thought had flashed through my mind also. Every gun of the whole party of Indians was leveled on us three. I shall never forget the picture, which left an impress that years cannot efface. The holes in those guns barrels looked as big as saucers.

I gave it only a glance, for my attention was drawn to something near at hand. A pressure on my shoulder was drawing me away from my husband. Looking back and up over my shoulder, I saw an Indian with an immense navy pistol trying to get a shot at my husband's head. Wrenching my arm from his grasp, I leaned over my husband, only to be roughly drawn aside. Another Indian stepped up, a pistol shot rang out, my husband's head fell back, and a red stream trickled down his face from beneath his hat. The warm sunshine, the smell of blood, the horror of it all, a faint remembrance of seeing rocks thrown at his head, my sister's screams, a sick faint feeling, and all was blank.[50]

Cowan, apparently only stunned by the head wound, regained consciousness and began hobbling back toward their original camp. He was discovered by another Indian driving a small horse herd and shot again, this time in the hip. He was finally rescued by troops and treated by army physicians who, according to Cowan, were more interested in seeing the geysers than caring for his wounds. At the time of his rescue Cowan still had the bullet that had knocked him senseless sticking out of his forehead just above his nose. His life was probably owed to wet powder or an improperly measured charge in the gun. Cowan was eventually reunited with his wife.

The only other member of the Radersburg party who was harmed was Oldham who was shot through the cheek while escaping. He also survived, although he lost two teeth.

The main body of Nez Perce crossed the Yellowstone to Pelican Creek leaving three small groups of warriors behind to cover their flank and to slow the army. They moved northeast ascending to the headwaters of the Lamar River. They then followed one of the Bannock Trail routes up Cache Creek and into the Clarks Fork drainage where Colonel Sturgis and the Seventh Cavalry waited.

In the Park near the Hayden Valley area were two other groups of tourists, the Earl of Dunraven, his friend Dr. George Kingsly, a guide named Texas Jack and a wrangler; and the Helena or Weikert party consisting of ten persons. Texas Jack discovered the Indians and escorted his party safely back to Mammoth Hot Springs, but he refused to warn the other party of the Indian presence. The Helena party eventually discovered the Indians, but did not leave the area. They camped that night on Otter Creek about three miles above the upper falls of the Yellowstone believing that there was no great danger and that they were hidden well enough. The next morning, as they lounged in camp, they were attacked by one of the three marauding bands left in the Park. One tourist was killed and one was wounded while the rest escaped unharmed, but they were split up, several eventually gathering at the crude hotel at Mammoth Hot Springs. Two of the group bolted from the camp and escaped into the timber. They headed overland to the west and, after 30 or 40 miles of grueling travel, hit the Madison Valley and some of Howard's supply wagons. They headed down the river to Virginia City after being fed by the soldiers. At the hotel at Mammoth, the hotel operator and the rest of the people there headed for Bozeman leaving five of the Helena party behind to search for their missing companions.

Meanwhile, the three Nez Perce warrior groups who remained behind to harass the civilians and military personnel in the Park roamed widely after attacking the Helena party. Even a ranch a mile or two north of present-day Gardiner, Montana, was looted and burned. Probably on their return from this last raid the Indians came by the Mammoth hotel, discovered three of the remaining members of the Helena party and killed one of them. These remaining Nez Perce warriors finally rejoined their families as the Indians descended onto the Plains east of the Park.

Gen. Howard, unaware that Gilbert had been dispatched to replace him, was now confident of success. The Nez Perce would be cut off by Sturgis's command and would be captured at last. There seemed to be no way out for the plucky group of Nez Perce who were now surrounded in the mountains by the best of the Indian-fighting army. Howard's route, after hacking a trail for his lumbering wagons and infantry through the central portion of the Park, was north of the Indians. He traveled up the Lamar River to Soda Butte Creek, over to the headwaters of Clarks Fork and down that river toward the waiting Sturgis.

Nez Perce scouts apparently detected Sturgis lying in wait along the lower Clarks Fork and advised their leaders of his location. The Indian leaders, still headed by Poker Joe, decided upon a simple plan which was perfectly conceived. Sturgis had not received information from his scouts or from Howard regarding the whereabouts of the Indians and was worried that they might exit the mountains via the Shoshone River to the south rather than down the nearly impassable Clarks Fork Canyon. The Nez Perce, in a well-executed move, made a highly visible start toward the Shoshone River, but then circled their ponies and doubled back to Clarks Fork and streamed down it and out onto the prairies while Sturgis and his troops moved south to the Shoshone River to block the Indians who never arrived. By the time Sturgis discovered his mistake and found the Nez Perce trail leading back to the Clarks Fork, Howard was already ahead of him and the Nez Perce were 50 miles ahead of Howard.

The End of the "Most Wonderful of Indian Wars"

The Indians headed down Clarks Fork, which soon turned toward its juncture with the Yellowstone River in Montana. The flight now was north to Canada, freedom and perhaps an alliance with Sitting Bull's Sioux. Shortly after crossing the Yellowstone west of Billings, they fought a skirmish with Sturgis's troops and escaped. Harassed by Crow and Bannock scouts riding in advance of the troops, the beleaguered Indians fled toward the Musselshell River, crossed it and traveled quickly on toward the Missouri. The Indians crossed the Missouri at Cow Island where they raided a steamboat freight depot for food and fought off soldiers stationed at the depot. Although Canada was now close, Looking Glass, who believed that pursuit by the soldiers had ceased, urged the bands to slow their pace to allow the families to rest. His advice was fatal this time.

Col. Nelson Miles crossed the Missouri at the mouth of the Mussel-shell in a forced march from Fort Keogh and learned of the Nez Perce route. Miles caught the Nez Perce camped at Snake Creek on the northern slopes of the Bear Paw Mountains 40 miles south of the Canadian border. The battle was intense and bloody, dragging on for six days. The Indians suffered terribly in the cold and from lack of food. Many of their chiefs, including Poker Joe, had been killed. Shortly after the death of Looking Glass, ironically the last Indian killed in the battle, Joseph rode to meet with Howard and Miles and gave his now famous surrender speech:

> Tell General Howard I know his heart. What he told me before, I have in my heart. I am tired of fighting. Our chiefs are killed. Looking Glass is dead. Toohoolhoolzote is dead. The old men are all dead. It is the young men who say yes and no. He who led on the young men is dead. It is cold and we have no blankets. The little children are freezing to death. My people, some of them, have run away to the hills and have no blankets, no food; no one knows where they are—perhaps freezing to death. I want to have time to look for my children and see how many I can find. Maybe I shall find them among the dead. Hear me my chiefs. I am tired; my heart is sick and sad. From where the sun now stands I will fight no more forever.[51]

The "wonderful," senseless war was over. Chief Joseph and 431 of the Nez Perce surrendered. About 330 escaped into Canada. Col. Miles demonstrated his respect for the Nez Perce in a letter to his wife by stating, "The fight was the most fierce of any Indian engagement I have ever been in. . . . The whole Nez Perce movement is unequalled in the history of Indian warfare."

The Fate of the Nez Perce

Following the war the fate of the Nez Perce paralleled that of other defeated Indians. It was a time of suffering and despair. Miles and Howard had promised the Nez Perce at the Bear Paws that they would return to their homes in Idaho and Oregon; instead they were shipped to Fort Leavenworth, Kansas, where they stayed until the summer of 1878 when they were moved to the Quapaw Indian Reserve in Kansas. In June of 1879 they were again relocated, this time to Tonkawa, Oklahoma, where they stayed until 1885 when they were finally allowed to return to the Northwest.

It was during this postwar period that Joseph rose to prominence. He tirelessly pursued the promises made by Miles to be allowed to return home. In January of 1879 he visited Washington, D.C., spoke to a gathering of members of Congress and the Cabinet and also met with the President of the United States. These efforts, coupled with the earlier media coverage of the war, elevated Joseph to a position of national prominence. Joseph's attempts to return his people to their homeland were complemented by his one-time enemy, Nelson Miles, who personally appealed to President Hayes on behalf of the Nez Perce. These combined efforts popularized the issue to the extent that it was supported by a number of eastern advocacy groups.

Finally, in 1885 Congress approved the return of the Nez Perce; however, the Commissioner of Indian Affairs argued convincingly that the settlers of the Wallowa Valley did not want Joseph's band to return because of several murders that occurred at the beginning of the war. As a result Joseph and his followers were sent to the Colville Reservation on Nespelem Creek in northeastern Washington while the remainder of the Nez Perce went home to Lapwai. Until his death Joseph appealed repeatedly to be allowed to return to his beloved Wallowa. All requests were denied. He died in 1904 in Nespelem while sitting in front of his tipi fire. The cause of death, according to the agency physician, was a broken heart.[52]

7

Indians and Yellowstone Geysers

Historians have had differences of opinion regarding the attitude of native peoples toward the geysers and hot springs found in Yellowstone Park.[53] Early reporters and explorers especially have stated unequivocally that the Indians feared the thermal features and avoided the Park. Col. P. W. Norris, Park superintendent from 1877–82, took this stand in his 1878 report to the Secretary of the Interior:

> Owing to the isolation of the park deep amid snowy mountains, and the superstitious awe of the roaring cataracts, sulphur pools, and spouting geysers over the surrounding pagan Indians, they seldom visit it, and only a few harmless Sheep-eater hermits, armed with bows and arrows, ever resided there, and even they are now vanished.[54]

More recently, scholars have maintained that Indians were not afraid of the geysers at all. A member of this group is Yellowstone Park historian Merrill Beal who wrote:

> While it is true that superstition and taboo loomed large in primitive experience there is no reason to suppose that Indians gave Wonderland a wide berth. Rather there is an abundance of material evidence that controverts this view. Futhermore, the proposition is at once illogical and untrue historically.[55]

These positions are at odds and it remains to examine the evidence used by both groups in order to attempt some reconciliation.

Evidence for Indian Responses to Yellowstone

The evidence falls into two categories: ethnohistoric/ethnographic and archæological. The former includes observations by early explorers of Indian behavior when confronted with the thermal actions and interviews with various Indians regarding their beliefs about the geysers and hot springs. The latter line of evidence depends on the occurrence of material items which accumulate in the areas where early people spent time camping or hunting.

While examining the evidence it is also important to consider specific details regarding the points critical to the issue. First of all, did Indians avoid the entire Yellowstone region or just a portion of it? Second, which geological features were the Indians afraid of? All of them, including the quiet hot pools, the mud pots, the geysers, and even the cataracts? Finally, who were the Indians who were supposed to have avoided these features? The Sheepeaters, the only permanent Park inhabitants, or the groups who occasionally traveled through Yellowstone on their trading and hunting trips?

The earliest report of Indian response to the geysers comes from W. A. Ferris who visited the Upper Geyser Basin in 1834. With him were two Indians of the Pend d'Oreille tribe who spoke a language related to, and who lived near, the Salish-speaking Flatheads of western Montana. Ferris reports that the Indians "were quite appalled, and could not by any means be induced to approach them (the geysers). . . . they believed them to be supernatural and supposed them to be the production of the Evil Spirit."[56] Another early record comes from Father DeSmet's travel journal dated to about 1850.

> The Indians pass these places (the geysers) in profound silence and with superstitious dread. They regard them as the abode of underground spirits always at war with one another, and continually at the anvil forging their weapons. They never pass without leaving some offering on a conspicuous point of the mysterious region.[57]

However, since De Smet did not personally visit Yellowstone, these impressions are secondhand and are not specific to the Indian groups affected. At a slightly earlier date Osbourne Russell encountered the Blackfeet on Pelican Creek near Yellowstone Lake in 1839 but did

Eruption of Giant Geyser in Yellowstone Park. (Photographer unknown, Photo Archives, Brigham Young University, Provo, Utah.)

not observe their reactions to the geysers. Some 25 years later Father Francis Xavier Kuppens was told of the wonders of Yellowstone by the Blackfeet, who eventually took the Father to Yellowstone Falls, Yellowstone Lake and the geysers in 1865. These two reports suggest the Blackfeet were familiar with the Park. Lt. Gustavus Doane and N. P. Langford both related encounters with the Crow near Tower Falls during their visit to the Park with the Washburn Party in 1870. Doane made a statement that "the larger tribes" did not enter the geyser basins on account of "superstitious ideas in connection with thermal springs" probably based on his communication with the Crows at this time.[58]

The reports of the Park's second superintendent, P. W. Norris, contain many references to Indian relics in the Park and the attitude of the Indians regarding the hot springs and geysers. Apparently Norris discussed this very topic with them. He quotes a Wind River Shoshone, Wesaw, as follows:

> He said that his people [Shoshones], the Bannocks, and Crows occasionally visited the Yellowstone Lake and River portions of the Park, but very seldom the geyser regions which he declared were "heap heap bad," and never wintered there, as white men sometimes did with horses.[59]

In 1882 Yellowstone was visited by Gen. Philip Sheridan who was guided by five Sheepeaters from the mountains south of Yellowstone Lake. Sheridan reports that these Indians had never visited the geyser basins and exhibited more astonishment and wonder at them than any of his group. He attributes their apparent previous avoidance of the geysers to superstition. Another late nineteenth-century report comes from Finn Burnett, a pioneer resident at the Wind River Reservation, who states that the Indians (probably the Wind River Shoshone) were much afraid of the geysers and never visited them.

Contrasting with these reports are those offered by Ake Hultkrantz who did anthropological fieldwork among the Plains or Wind River Shoshone in 1948. His informants state that indeed the Shoshone did believe the geysers contained spirits and prayed to them and some avoided or hurried past the geysers on their visits. Others, however, though scared at first by the "steaming waters" discovered it was just water. They then undressed and bathed in the waters that went "up

Hot pool at the summit of Jupiter Terrace, Yellowstone Park. (Photograph by Gifford, Photo Archives, Brigham Young University, Provo, Utah.)

and down." The bathing may have been for medicinal purposes according to Hultkrantz.

Another Shoshone informant of Hultkrantz told his grandfather who was for a time a member of a Sheepeater band that spent summers in Yellowstone. The Tavonasia band, as they were called, camped near the geysers in the Firehole Basin, bathed in the geysers and prayed to their spirits. However, this informant stated emphatically that of all the warriors of Washakie's band (the Wind River Shoshone) only the Tavonasia band hunted there.

Also in contrast, in 1935 two veterans of the 1877 Nez Perce War, Many Wounds and White Hawk, revisited the Park. Asked about fear of the geysers and hot springs they said that they were not afraid and implied that the Nez Perce, during their earlier visits to the Park, took advantage of the hot water by using it for cooking.

In weighing this line of evidence against the questions stated earlier it seems apparent for the most part that the neighboring or local Indians were not strangers to the Yellowstone region and almost all were aware of the more spectacular thermal features in the major geyser basins. As to whether the Indians were more afraid of the hot springs or the geysers, the evidence is not clear but does suggest that only the active geysers, which were seen as containing spirits, awed the Indians. With respect to the final questions, "Who were the Indians who were afraid of the thermal features?" there does seem to be a general tendency, as Hultkrantz points out, for the local Sheep-eaters to be less apprehensive about the geysers than those Indians who only occasionally visited the Park. However, as we have seen, the reactions varied from individual to individual.

The archæological evidence is much less controversial. Norris in 1880 reports that decaying Sheepeater habitation structures were "abundant near Mammoth Hot Springs, the various fire-hole basins, the shores of Yellowstone Lake, the newly explored Hoodoo Region, and in nearly all of the sheltered glens and valleys of the Park." Norris's 1881 report also contains many references to driveways and miscellaneous artifacts collected in Yellowstone, though he does not mention their provenience.[60]

Archæological reconnaissance work by the University of Montana in the late 1950s and early 1960s, combined with earlier work, identi-fied nearly 500 prehistoric archæological sites in Yellowstone. Much of the Park is still to be surveyed.[61] These sites included several in the Norris Geyser Basin and several in the Lower and Upper Geyser basins, even though considerable disturbance and collecting had already taken place. It must be mentioned again that the majority of these archæological finds date earlier than the Shoshone-speaking Sheepeaters who arrived in the vicinity probably as recently as the 1800s.[62]

The archæological and ethnohistorical/ethnographic evidence point to conclusions which now appear fairly obvious. The Yellow-stone region as we know it was certainly not avoided by Indians. It is possible that certain groups or individuals avoided the more active thermal features as might be predicted in light of what we now know about the beliefs of Plains and the Great Basin Indian people. In the Basin, spirits such as water babies were commonly thought to live in the water. These spirits held tremendous power, but it was power which could work for or against an individual at the whim of the spirit. Though many feared this power, some sought it for success in hunting or shamanistic practices. Also, warriors of the Plains tribes sought success in war and hunting through a quest for the power of various spirits via visions and dreams and went to places known to be the haunts of spirits to obtain power. As a result the geysers, while being held in awe by most and avoided by some, may have actually acted as a magnet for the ambitious. The various responses to the geysers by different Indians within the same group can be explained in part by the highly individualized nature of both Plains and Great Basin societies and the lack of a uniform or highly structured belief system. The simplistic generalization that all Indians were afraid of the unique geological phenomena in Yellowstone also fits with pre-conceived notions about "primitive" groups and their propensity to attribute the strange or unusual to the supernatural.

M. Beal explains P. W. Norris's endorsement of the Indian's fear of Yellowstone as "an adaptation of business psychology to a promising national resort." In other words, Norris chose to reassure potential tourists who might fear the danger of Indian attack after the Nez Perce War and the attack on the Radersburg tourists by maintaining that Yellowstone was avoided by all Indians. Norris may have simply found this an expedient way to improve the image of Yellowstone.

Epilogue

After the Nez Perce War of 1877 and the Bannock War of 1878, any real Indian presence in Yellowstone came to an end. The area's new status as a national park and the importance of tourist visitation demanded that the Park be kept free of any threat of Indian hostilities or even the possibility of such a threat. As a result, the very effective campaign to characterize the Park as taboo to the "superstitious" indigenous peoples was launched. That characterization was clearly in error, however. The American Indian knew of the wonders of Yellowstone thousands of years ago. The tendency for Europeans to believe that they were the first to be spellbound by the thundering falls, steaming geysers and fumeroles and scenic beauty of the region is an example of ethnocentrism. Several archaeological studies in and around Yellowstone demonstrate that the first visits to the Park began with the dawn of North American prehistory. Distinctive artifacts and other clues argue that through all the periods of man's history in the New World Yellowstone was part of a territory whose resources were known and used by early people.

We will never know the thoughts of prehistoric man as he watched Old Faithful eject its eternal spray or peered through shifting banks of steam into the richly hued depths of the boiling springs, but we do know that obsidian from the Park found its way thousands of miles eastward into the economic and religious life of the Hopewell Indians, and was undoubtedly used by many groups in between. We also know that the Park was a hunting, fishing and gathering area for prehistoric peoples for centuries. With the turning of the seasons these people moved through the high country in pursuit of game, roots, seeds, nuts and other commodities. After a day's activities, they probably sat around the evening fire and told and retold the centuries-old tales of hunting successes and failures. Yellowstone was home to them. They knew it in a way no modern man ever will.

The evidence, given to us through careful archaeological study and diverse historical accounts, enhances our appreciation of the role of Yellowstone in the cultural development of North America. When viewed from the perspective of the Park's 10,000-year cultural history, our share of the heritage is miniscule, and it becomes clear that we have only begun to truly understand the unique and enduring allure of Yellowstone.

Notes

1. William R. Keefer, "The Geologic Story of Yellowstone National Park," United States Geological Survey Bulletin No. 1347 (Washington D.C.: G.P.O., 1972).

2. Joseph Paxson Iddings, "Obsidian Cliff, Yellowstone National Park," United States Geological Survey, Seventh Annual Report (Washington, D.C.: G.P.O., 1883), pp. 261–62.

3. Aubrey L. Haines, *The Yellowstone Story*, vol. 1 (Yellowstone National Park: Yellowstone Library and Museum Association, 1977), p. 16.

4. Larry Lahren, "Bone Foreshafts from a Clovis Burial in Southwestern Montana," *Science* (October 1974): 147–50.

5. Harold McCracken, comp., *The Mummy Cave Project in Northwestern Wyoming* (Cody, Wyoming: Buffalo Bill Historical Center, 1978).

6. Dee C. Taylor, *Preliminary Archaeological Investigations in Yellowstone National Park*, manuscript on file, Yellowstone National Park Archives, Mammoth, Wyoming, 1964.

7. Aubrey L. Haines, "Preliminary Report on the Rigler Bluffs Prehistoric Indian Site, 24PA401," manuscript on file, Yellowstone National Park Archives, 1962.

8. Jesse D. Jennings, *Prehistory of North America* (New York: McGraw-Hill, 1974), p. 228.

9. James B. Griffen, A. A. Gordus and G. A. Wright, "Identification of Hopewellian Obsidian in the Middle West," *American Antiquity* 34, no. 1 (1969): 1–14. For additional information on the yellow obsidian blades from Hopewell Mounds illustrated in the text, see W. K. Moorehead, "The Hopewell Mound Group of Ohio," *Field Museum of Natural History, Publication 211, Anthropological Series*, vol. 6, no. 5 (Chicago: Field Museum of Natural History, 1922).

10. The reference for Yellowstone obsidian in Iowa is Duane C. Anderson, Joseph A. Tiffany and Fred W. Nelson, "Recent Research on Obsidian from Iowa Archaeological Sites," *American Antiquity* 51, no. 4 (1986) :837–52. For North Dakota, Fred W. Nelson, personal communication, 1986. For Oklahoma, Griffen et al., 1969.

11. George C. Frison, *The Wardell Buffalo Trap 48SU301: Communal Procurement in the Upper Green River Basin, Wyoming*, Anthropological Papers No. 48 (Ann Arbor: Museum of Anthropology, University of Michigan, 1973), p. 74.

12. Taylor, *Preliminary Archaeological Investigations*, pp. 70-73.

13. Gary A. Wright, "The Shoshonean Migration Problem," *Plains Anthropologist* 23, no. 80 (1978) :113–36.

14. Francis Haines, "Northward Spread of Horses to the Plains Indians," *American Anthropologist* 40, no. 3 (1938), pp. 429–37.

15. John C. Ewers, *The Blackfeet, Raiders on the Northwestern Plains* (Norman: University of Oklahoma Press, 1958), p. 7.

16. Bernard DeVoto, ed., *The Journals of Lewis and Clark* (Boston: Houghton Mifflin Co., 1953), pp. 435–40.

17. Osbourne Russell, *Journal of a Trapper*, edited by Aubrey L. Haines (Lincoln: University of Nebraska Press), pp. 101–2.

18. Ewers, *The Blackfeet*, p. 66.

19. John C. Ewers, *The Horse in Blackfoot Indian Culture*, Smithsonian Institution Bureau of American Ethnology Bulletin 159 (Washington, D.C.: G.P.O., 1955), p. 8.

20. Edwin Thompson Denig, *Five Indian Tribes of the Upper Missouri* (Norman: University of Oklahoma Press, 1961), p. 65.

21. Orrin H. and Lorraine Bonny, *Battle Drums and Geysers* (Chicago: The Swallow Press, 1970), p. 65.

22. Sidney M. Lamb, "Linguistic Prehistory in the Great Basin," *International Journal of American Linguistics* 24, no. 2 (1958) : 95–100, and David B. Madsen, "Dating Paiute-Shoshone Expansion in the Great Basin," *American Antiquity* 40, no. 1 (1975) : 391–405. For more complete recent histories of the Shoshone and Bannock, see Brigham D. Madsen, *The Lemhi: Sacajawea's People* (Caldwell, Idaho: Caxton Press, 1979) ; Brigham D. Madsen, *The Northern Shoshoni* (Caldwell, Idaho: Caxton Press, 1980) ; and Robert F. and Yolanda Murphy, *Shoshone-Bannock Subsistence and Society*, University of California Anthropological Papers, vol. 16, no. 7 (Berkeley: University of California Press, 1960), pp. 293-338.

23. For some discussion of the origins of the term Snake, see Brigham D. Madsen, *The Bannock of Idaho* (Caldwell, Idaho: Caxton Press, 1958), p. 19; Virginia Cole Trenholm and Maurice Carley, *The Shoshonis, Sentinels of the Rockies* (Norman: University of Oklahoma Press, 1964), pp. 3–4.

24. Julian H. Steward, *Basin-Plateau Aboriginal Sociopolitical Groups*, Bureau of American Ethnology Bulletin No. 120 (Washington, D.C.: G.P.O., 1938), p. 186.

25. See Madsen, *The Bannock of Idaho*, p. 18; Steward, *Basin-Plateau*, p. 198; and Sven Liljeblad, "Indian Peoples in Idaho," manuscript on file, Idaho State University, Pocatello, p. 82, for additional discussion of the origin and meaning of the term Bannock.

26. Liljeblad, "Indian Peoples in Idaho," p. 61.

27. Steward, *Basin-Plateau*, p. 186.

28. Ake Hultkrantz, "The Shoshones in the Rocky Mountain Area," *Annals of Wyoming* 33, no. 1 (1961): 34.

29. Gary Wright, "The Shoshonean Migration Problem," *Plains Anthropologist*, vol. 23, no. 80 (1978): 113.

30. Washington Irving, "Astoria," in *The Works of Washington Irving*, vol. 2 (New York: Peter Fenelon Collier, Publisher, n.d.), p. 370.

31. Cited in David Dominick, "The Sheepeaters," *Annals of Wyoming* 36, no. 20 (1964): 132–68.

32. Russell, *Journal of a Trapper*, p. 26.

33. Philetus W. Norris, "Annual Report of the Superintendent of the Yellowstone National Park," in Annual Report of the Secretary of the Interior on the Operations of the Department for the Year Ended June 30, 1880, Vol. II (Washington, D.C.: G.P.O., 1880), p. 605.

34. Ake Hultkrantz, cited in Taylor, *Preliminary Archaeological Investigations in Yellowstone National Park*, p. 33.

35. Liljeblad, "Indian Peoples in Idaho," p. 61.

36. Dominick, "The Sheepeaters," p. 140.

37. See, for example, George C. Frison, *Prehistoric Hunters of the High Plains* (New York: Academic Press, 1978), p. 75.

38. Liljeblad, "Indian Peoples in Idaho," p. 97.

39. Ibid., p. 96.

40. Dominick, "The Sheepeaters," p. 162.

41. Norris, "Annual Report . . . for 1880," p. 606.

42. Frison, *Prehistoric Hunters*, p. 264.

43. Liljeblad, "Indian Peoples in Idaho," p. 97.

44. See Murphy and Murphy, *Shoshone-Bannock Subsistence and Society*, p. 310.

45. Cited in Madsen, *The Lemhi*, p. 104.

46. Russell, *Journal of a Trapper*, p. 123.

47. Liljeblad, "Indian Peoples in Idaho," pp. 63–65.

48. For more information on the Bannock Trail see Wayne F. Replogle, *Yellowstone's Bannock Indian Trails* (Yellowstone National Park: Yellowstone Library and Museum Association, 1956); and Aubrey L. Haines, *The Bannock Indian Trail* (Yellowstone National Park: Yellowstone Library and Museum Association, 1964).

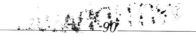

49. Mark H. Brown, "Yellowstone Tourists and the Nez Perce," *Montana Magazine of Western History* 16, no. 3 (1966) : 34.

50. Paul Schullery, "Mrs. George Cowan 1877," in *Old Yellowstone Days* (Boulder: Associated University Press, 1979), pp. 11–12.

51. This poetic statement apparently made by Joseph at the time of surrender is printed in many places. For some well-researched discussion of the details of the Nez Perce War see Mark H. Brown, *The Flight of the Nez Perce* (New York: G. P. Putnam Sons, 1967); and Alvin Josephy, *The Nez Perce and the Opening of the Northwest* (New Haven: Yale University Press, 1965).

52. Again be referred to Josephy, *The Nez Perce and the Opening of the Northwest*, especially the Epilogue, for excellent coverage of the postwar period and Joseph's efforts. The speech made by Joseph to Congress in 1879 is every bit as stirring as his "Fight No More Forever" speech and is worth reading.

53. For an excellent discussion of the perception of Yellowstone's geysers by Indians and to which considerable is owed for this discussion see Ake Hultkrantz, "The Fear of Geysers among Indians of the Yellowstone Park Area," in *Lifeways of Intermountain and Plains Montana Indians*, edited by Leslie B. Davis (Bozeman, Montana: Montana State University, 1979), pp. 33–42.

54. Philetus W. Norris, "Report on the Yellowstone National Park . . . for the year 1877" (Washington, D.C.: G.P.O., 1878), p. 842.

55. Merrill D. Beal, *The Story of Man in Yellowstone* (Yellowstone: Yellowstone Library Museum Association, 1960), p. 328.

56. W. A. Ferris, *Life in the Rocky Mountains 1830–1835* (Salt Lake City: Rocky Mountain Bookshop, 1940), pp. 205–6.

57. Cited in Hultkrantz, "The Fear of Geysers," p. 35.

58. Bonney and Bonney, *Battle Drums and Geysers*, p. 334.

59. Philetus W. Norris, "Fifth Annual Report of the Superintendent of the Yellowstone National Park," Report of the Secretary of the Interior, 47th Congr., 1st Sess. (Washington, D.C.: G.P.O., 1882), p. 782.

60. Norris, "Annual Report . . . for 1880," p. 606; Taylor, *Preliminary Archaeological Investigations in Yellowstone National Park*, p. 46–49.

61. Taylor, *Preliminary Archaeological Investigations in Yellowstone Park*, p. 100.

62. Wright, "The Shoshone Migration Problem," p. 113.